Crazy for Crochet

Crazy for Crochet

LILLY SECILIE BRANDAL

BENTE MYHRER

TRAFALGAR SQUARE
North Pomfret, Vermont

First published in the United States of America
in 2016 by
Trafalgar Square Books
North Pomfret, Vermont 05053

Originally published in Norwegian as Heklelyst.

ISBN: 978-1-57076-759-3

Library of Congress Control Number: 2015956881

DESIGN
Laila Mjøs *Blæst

PHOTOGRAPHY
May B. Langhelle

CROCHET SCHOOL ILLUSTRATIONS
Laila Mjøs, Ingunn Cecilie Jensen, Ingse Revold

TRANSLATION
Carol Huebscher Rhoades

Printed in China
10 9 8 7 6 5 4 3 2 1

Dear friends of crochet,

In this book, you'll find dozens of great crochet patterns. The projects vary considerably—from clothing, toys, and accessories to items for babies and children, as well as pretty sweaters and cardigans for women, to inspiring projects for interior design, hats, scarves, mittens and slippers. You'll also find a detailed course in crochet with clear drawings and explanations of all the basic stitches and techniques for crochet. If you are a beginner, among other things, it is important to become familiar with the abbreviations we use in this book.

Crochet, like knitting, has had both up- and down- turns. From 1960 to 1980, crochet was a very popular hobby. People crocheted hats, cardigans, coats, bags, rugs, tablecloths, lace collars, curtains, and bedcovers. There was almost nothing one couldn't crochet! After a lull, crochet has become popular again, and in 2014 it really took off. We saw a new focus on crochet thanks in large part to the Olympic hat from Sochi—all of Norway was smitten with crochet fever! Young girls and even boys were seen with crochet hooks in their hands. This new interest also became an important source of inspiration for the two of us.

We have both been in the yarn industry for many years. Bente Myhrer has run her yarn shop, Bente's Boutique, since 1969. She established her first shop on Bjølsen, now the longest running yarn store in Oslo. After a few years, she opened a new shop on Carl Berner Place. That was followed by shops on Markveie in Grünerløkka, on Dokka in Oppland, and in the shopping center of Østerås in Bærum (the last two shops in this list are now closed). Since 1986, Lilly Secilie Brandal has been working in Bente's Boutique, first on Markveien, then in the branch on Bjølsen, now called Strikkelilly, where she manages the shop with a great deal of enthusiasm and personal engagement. We've had a close working relationship all these years, and have designed new crochet and knitting patterns, both for our shops and for large yarn companies in Norway and Sweden. Many of our designs have also appeared in weekly magazines and newspapers. We have traveled—and continue to travel—to many trade fairs. The trips to Sweden, Denmark, Germany, and not least France and Paris, have given us so much

inspiration. We are always on the lookout for good ideas and especially for various yarns and accessories that will capture our customers' interest.

Those of us in the yarn industry are most concerned with ensuring that our customers and potential new customers will be inspired to engage in handcrafts and sustain our Norwegian traditions. With today's rapid tempo, everything has to be so fast, but working with handcrafts is not—and we think it is important to do some things more slowly. With peace and quiet for our souls, life becomes a bit easier to live. It is not always what you make that is most important, but finding that quiet space where your fingers can work completely by themselves.

We hope that we have managed to make a varied book that will be suitable for both beginners and more experienced crocheters, and we wish you many fine and quiet moments with the crochet hook and yarn ball.

If you have problems with any of our patterns, or there is something you have a question about, you can contact us at one of our shops.

You'll find Lilly at Strikkelilly
Yarn and Embroidery,
Gjøvik St 1, on Bjølsen at Sagene, Oslo.
Telephone: 011 47 22 18 26 39

You can meet Bente at Bente's Boutique,
Christian Michelsen St 1,
on Carl Berner Place, Oslo.
Telephone: 011 47 22 37 44 86

You can also send questions to:
strikkelilly@gmail.com

You'll find everything you need for all the crochet patterns in this book or for making your own designs in our shops.

Good luck!

Lilly and Bente

Contents

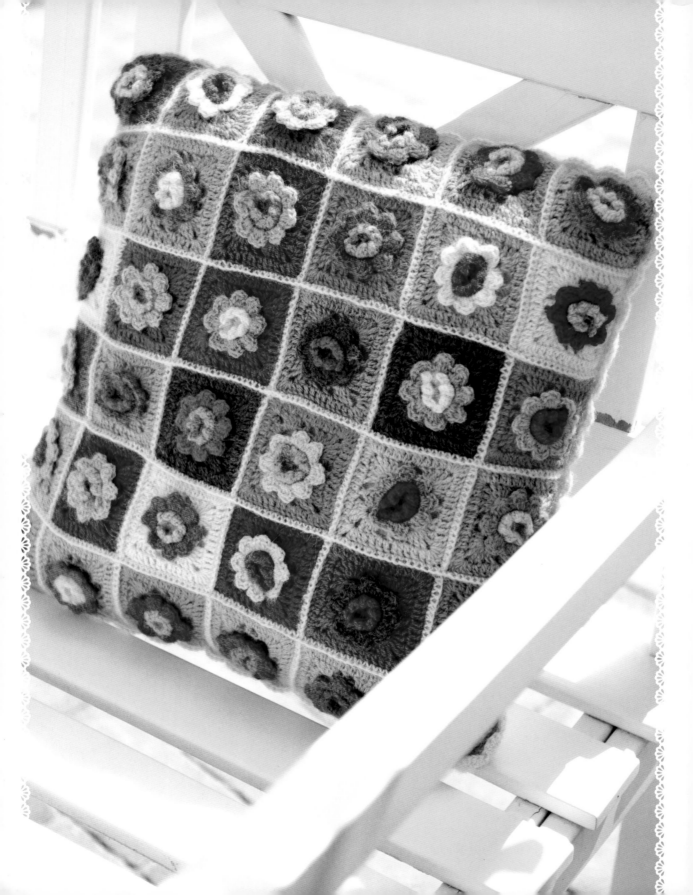

Pillow with Flower Squares

THIS DESIGN CAN ALSO BE USED FOR A BABY BLANKET, A CARRIAGE THROW, OR A BIG COVERLET. IT IS THE SQUARE ITSELF WHICH IS THE INSPIRATION SO YOU CAN DECIDE WHAT YOU WANT FOR A FINISHED PRODUCT.

Yarn: We've used a number of colors of various sizes of fine alpaca yarn. The yarns do not all have to be exactly the same size.
Crochet Hook: U.S. D-3 / 3 mm
Finished Measurements: 17¾ x 17¾ in / 45 x 45 cm
The cover consists of 36 blocks sewn together, 6 across and 6 down.

Begin with a magic ring (see page 147).

Rnd 1: Ch 4 (= the 1st dc + 1 ch), (1 dc around loop, ch 1) 7 times and end with 1 sl st into 3rd ch at beg of rnd = 8 ch loops. Tighten magic ring.

Rnd 2: Change colors. *1 sl st, 1 hdc, 1 dc, 1 hdc, 1 sl st) around each ch loop. End with 1 sl st into 1st st.

Rnd 3: Change colors and attach new color with 1 sl st behind the 1st dc of Rnd 1. Ch 5 (= 1 dc + 2 ch), (1 dc behind next dc, ch 2) around. End with 1 sl st into 3rd ch (= 8 ch loops).

Rnd 4: (1 hdc, 1 dc, 1 tr, 1 dc, 1 hdc) in each ch loop around. End with 1 sl st into 1st hdc.

Rnd 5: Change colors. Attach new color with 1 sl st into 1st dc of Rnd 3. Ch 6 (= 1st dc + 3 ch), (1 dc in next dc, ch 3) around. End with 1 sl st into top of 3rd ch (= 8 ch loops).

Rnd 6: Ch 4 (= 1 tr), 1 tr, 2 dc, ch 1, 1 dc in next ch loop, ch 1, *(2 dc, 2 tr, ch 1, 2 tr, 2 dc) in next ch loop = corner; ch 1, 1 dc in next ch loop, ch 1; rep from * around, ending with 2 dc, 2 tr, ch 1, 1 sl st into top of ch 4.

Rnd 7: Ch 3 (= 1st dc), 2 dc in ch loop and then work 1 dc in each st of previous round, but, at each corner, work 5 dc in ch 1 loop. End with 2 dc in ch loop, 1 sl st into top of ch 3.

Finishing
Place 2 squares together with RS facing out. Crochet the squares together with sc so that there is a raised edge. Continue joining squares until there are 6 squares across. Make 5 more rows of squares the same way and then join all the rows for a 6 x 6 square block.

Make a fan edging around the pillow cover as follows: Begin 2 sts from one corner and work 1 sc, skip 1 sc, *5 dc, skip 1 sc, secure fan with 1 sc, skip 1 sc*; rep from * to * around. The fans may not be evenly distributed around so do the best you can to arrange the fans along each side.

Weave in all ends.

Tip
If you want to avoid weaving in all the ends at the very last moment, carry and cover the yarn ends when working the first round after adding or cutting the yarn.

Pillow with flower squares

Large Doily

IF YOU WORK ALL THE ROUNDS OF THIS PATTERN, YOU'LL HAVE A DOILY FOR A TABLE OR BOWL. IF YOU DECIDE TO END WITH ROUND 6, THE DOILY WILL FIT NICELY UNDER A SMALL BOWL OR PLATE.

Yarn: 50 g Fiol from Solberg Spinderi (CYCA #2 [sport/baby], 100% mercerized cotton, 185 yd/169 m / 50 g)
Crochet Hook: U.S. size C-2 / 2.5 mm
Finished Measurements: approx. 13¾ in / 35 cm in diameter

Ch 8 and join into a ring with 1 sl st into 1st ch.

Rnd 1: Ch 1, work 11 sc around ring; end with 1 sl st into 1st ch = 12 sc.

Rnd 2: Ch 5 (= 1 dc + 2 ch), (1 dc in next st, ch 2) around. End with 1 sl st into the 3rd ch at beg of rnd = 12 dc + 12 ch loops around.

Rnd 3: 1 sl st into ch loop, ch 8 (= 1 tr + 4 ch), (1 tr in next ch loop, ch 4) around. End with 1 sl st into 4th ch at beg of rnd = 12 ch loops.

Rnd 4: 1 sl st into 1st ch loop, ch 4 (= 1 tr). Work 5 tr in same ch loop = 6 tr. (Ch 4, 1 sc in next ch loop, ch 4, 6 tr in next ch loop) around, ending with ch 4, 1 sc in next ch loop, ch 4, 1 sl st into top of ch 4 at beg of rnd.

Rnd 5: Ch 4 (= 1 tr), 2 tr in 2nd tr, 1 tr in 3rd tr, 1 tr in 4th tr, 2 tr in 5th tr, 1 tr in 6th tr, ch 12, (work 8 tr distributed over trebles in sequence just described, with the first tr in the first tr of set of tr below, ch 12) around. End with 1 sl st into top of ch 4 at beg of rnd.

Rnd 6: Sl st in each st to 4th tr, (1 sc between the 4th and 5th tr, 23 tr in the ch-12 loop) around. End with 1 sl st into 4th tr. The small doily ends here.

Rnd 7: Sl st in each st to 6th tr. [Ch 6, skip 5 tr, 1 dtr + ch 6 + 1 dtr in next tr (= center tr), ch 6, skip 5 tr, 1 sc in next tr, ch 11, 1 sc in 6th tr of next ch loop with 23 tr] around, ending with ch 6, skip 5 tr, 1 dtr + ch 6, 1 dtr in next tr (= center tr), ch 6, skip 5 tr, 1 sc in next tr, ch 11, 1 sl st into 1st ch.

Rnd 8: Sl st in each st to 1st ch-6 loop. [11 tr (begin rnd with ch 4, 10 tr) in the ch-6 loop, ch 10, 1 dtr + ch 3 + 1 dtr in the 6th of the 11 ch, ch 10] around. End with 1 sl st into 4th ch at beg of rnd.

Rnd 9: Ch 5 (= 1 tr + 1 ch), 1 tr in each tr + ch 1 between each tr, (ch 7, 3 tr + ch 2 + 3 tr in ch-3 loop, ch 7, 1 tr in each tr and ch 1 between each dc) around, ending with ch 7, 3 tr + ch 2, + 3 tr in ch loop, ch 7, 1 sl st into 4th ch at beg of rnd.

Rnd 10: Ch 6 (= 1 tr + 2 ch), 1 tr in each tr with ch 2 between each tr, (ch 5, 3 tr + ch 2 + 3 tr in ch-2 loop, ch 5, 1 tr in each tr and ch 2 between each tr) around, ending with ch 5, 3 tr + ch 2, + 3 tr in ch loop, ch 5, 1 sl st into 4th ch at beg of rnd.

Rnd 11: (1 sc in 1st tr, ch 8, 1 sc between 3rd and 4th tr, ch 4, 4 dtr in space between 5th and 6th tr, ch 4, 4 dtr in space between 6th and 7th tr, ch 4, 1 sc between 8th and 9th tr, ch 8, 1 sc in last tr, ch 6, 3 tr + ch 2, + 3 tr in ch-2 loop, ch 6) around. End with 1 sl st into 1st tr.

Cut yarn and fasten off.
Lightly steam press doily.

Small Doily from an Old Bedcover Pattern

OLD BEDCOVERS WERE CROCHETED WITH FINE YARN AND SMALL CROCHET HOOKS. TODAY WE USE HEAVIER YARN AND BIGGER HOOKS AND CAN BE SATISFIED WITH JUST ONE MOTIF FOR A NICE DOILY.

Yarn: 50 g Fiol from Solberg Spinderi (CYCA #2 [sport/baby], 100% mercerized cotton, 185 yd/169 m / 50 g)

Crochet Hook: U.S. size C-2 / 2.5 mm

Finished Measurements: approx. 9½ in / 24 cm in diameter

Ch 10 and join into a ring with 1 sl st into 1st ch (or begin with a magic ring—see page 147 in the Crochet School section).

Rnd 1: Ch 4, work 23 tr around ring and end with 1 sl st into top of ch 4 at beg of rnd = 24 tr.

Rnd 2: Ch 3, skip 1 tr, 1 dc between the 2nd and 3rd tr, ch 6, 1 dc between the 2 sts crossed between the ch loop and st (= 1 crossed dc), ch 4, [2 loops around hook, insert hook between the 2 next tr and yoh, bring yarn through 2 loops, yoh, skip 2 tr, yoh, yarn through 2 loops 4 times (with 1 yoh each time), ch 6, 1 dc through the 2 sts in the cross between the ch loop and dc, ch 4] around, ending with 1 sl st into 3rd ch at beg of rnd = 8 crossed dc with ch-4 loop between each.

Rnd 3: Ch 1, (4 sc in each of the 16 ch loops (large and small) around and end with 1 sl st into the 1st ch = 64 sc.

Rnds 4–11: Begin with ch 1, and then work 1 sc through both loops in each st around. End with 1 sl st into 1st ch. **NOTE:** On Rnds 7 and 9, increase 8 sts evenly spaced around = 80 sts.

Rnd 12: Ch 4 (= 1 dc, 1 ch), (1 dc in next sc, ch 1) around = 80 dc with 1 ch between each dc. End with 1 sl st into 3rd ch at beg of rnd.

Rnd 13: Ch 3, skip 2 dc, work 1 dc between the 2nd and 3rd dc, ch 6, 1 dc between the 2 sts of cross between ch loop and dc (= 1 crossed dc), ch 5, [2 loops around hook, skip 2 dc, insert hook between the two next dc and 1 yoh, bring yarn through 2 loops, yoh, skip 2 dc, insert hook between the two next dc, 1 yoh, bring yarn through 2 loops 4 times with 1 yoh each time, ch 6, 1 dc through 2 sts in cross between ch loop and dc, ch 5] around, ending with 1 sl st into 3rd ch at beg of rnd = 20 crossed dc with 5 ch between each.

Rnd 14: 1 sl st into 1st ch loop, ch 6, 1 dc in same ch loop, [ch 3, 1 sc in ch-5 loop, ch 3, (1 dc, ch 3, 1 dc) in ch loop of the crossed st] around, ending with ch 3, 1 sl st into 3rd ch at beg of rnd.

Rnd 15: 1 sl st into 1st ch-3 loop, ch 6, 1 dc in same ch loop, [ch 5, 1 sc in sc of previous rnd, ch 5, (1 dc, ch 3, 1 dc) in ch-3 loop] around, ending with ch 5, 1 sc in sc, ch 5, 1 sl st into 3rd ch at beg of rnd.

Cut yarn and fasten off.

Yarn Basket

SIMPLY SAID, THIS IS A BASKET MADE OF YARN FOR YARN. IF YOU WANT A FIRMER BASKET, USE A HOOK ONE SIZE SMALLER.

Yarn: Hubro from Dale Garn (CYCA #6 [bulky/roving], 100% wool, 72 yd/66 m / 100 g), approx. 500 g Color 1, Green, 100 g Color 2, Light Blue (or leftovers of another yarn)
Crochet Hook: U.S. size K-10½ or L-11 / 7 mm
Finished Measurements: *From base to top (excluding the picot edging):* approx. 13¾ in / 35 cm; *circumference:* approx. 31½ in / 80 cm

The basket is worked from side to side with short rows to shape the basket.

NOTE: Always work single crochet (sc) through the back loop only. Start each new row with ch 1 = 1st sc.

With Color 1, ch 41.

Row 1: Insert hook into the 2nd ch from hook and work 40 sc.

Row 2: Insert hook into the 2nd sc from hook and work in sc across until 3 sts rem; turn.

Row 3: Sc across.

Row 4: Sc across until 3 sts rem before previous short row turn; turn.

Row 5: Sc across.

Row 6: Work as for Row 4.

Row 7: Sc across.

Row 8: Sc across, including the "stair steps" of the short rows = 40 sc.
Repeat Rows 3–8 to finished measurements. End with Row 8.

Finishing
Weave in all ends. Crochet (or sew) the short sides together. Weave yarn through the hole at the base and pull tight; fasten off.

PICOT EDGING

Rnd 1: Change to Color 2. Begin with 1 rnd sc around top edge of basket; end with 1 sl st to 1st st.

Rnd 2: (Ch 3, 1 sc in 1st ch, skip 1 st, 1 sc in next st) around.

Weave in all ends on WS.

Throw Rug

FINE COLORS HARMONIZE IN THIS MAT WITH THE COLORS CHANGING ON EVERY ROUND. IF YOU WANT A BIGGER MAT, JUST KEEP INCREASING AS DESCRIBED IN THE PATTERN. ADD A NON-SKID UNDERLAY FOR USE AS A FLOOR MAT.

Yarn: Hubro from Dale Garn (CYCA #6 [bulky/roving], 100% wool, 72 yd/66 m / 100 g)
Yarn Amounts: 100 g of each color:
Color 1: Light Gray
Color 2: Old Rose
Color 3: White
Color 4: Yellow
Color 5: Light Blue
Color 6: Gray-Green
Color 7: Pearl Pink
Color 8: Beige
Crochet Hook: U.S. size L-11 / 8 mm
Finished Measurements: Diameter, approx. 27½ in / 70 cm

NOTE: Begin each round with ch 3 (= 1st dc) and end each rnd with 1 sl st into top of ch 3, using next color in sequence.

With Color 1, ch 6 and close into a ring with 1 sl st into 1st ch.

Rnd 1: Ch 3, 11 dc around ring = 12 dc; end with 1 sl st into top of ch 3.

Rnd 2 (Color 2): Ch 3, 1 dc in next st, (2 dc in each st around) = 24 dc; end with 1 sl st into top of ch 3.

Rnd 3 (Color 3): Ch 3, 1 dc in next st, (1 dc in next st, 2 dc in next st) around, end with 1 dc = 36 dc. End with 1 sl st into top of ch 3.

Rnd 4 (Color 4): Ch 3, 1 dc in next st, (1 dc in of next 2 sts, 2 dc in next st) around, end with 2 dc = 48 dc. End with 1 sl st into top of ch 3.

Rnd 5 (Color 5): Ch 3, 1 dc in next st, (1 dc in of next 3 sts, 2 dc in next st) around, end with 3 dc = 60 dc. End with 1 sl st into top of ch 3.

Rnd 6 (Color 6): Ch 3, 1 dc in next st, (1 dc in of next 4 sts, 2 dc in next st) around, end with 4 dc = 72 dc. End with 1 sl st into top of ch 3.

Rnd 7 (Color 7): Ch 3, 1 dc in next st, (1 dc in of next 5 sts, 2 dc in next st) around, end with 5 dc = 84 dc. End with 1 sl st into top of ch 3.

Rnd 8 (Color 8): Ch 3, 1 dc in next st, (1 dc in of next 6 sts, 2 dc in next st) around, end with 6 dc = 96 dc. End with 1 sl st into top of ch 3.
Repeat Rnds 1–8 in the same color sequence, with 1 st more between increases on each round and 1 more dc at end of rnd = 12 sts increased on each rnd.

PICOT EDGING
Attach Color 1 with 1 sl st, (1 sc, ch 3, 1 sc in 1st ch, skip 1 st, 1 sc in next st) around.
Weave in all ends on WS.

Tip
This is a good basic pattern that can also be used for anything from round potholders to pillow backings. It can be worked with fine or heavy yarn and in one or more colors.

Cozy Coverlet

GRANNY SQUARES ARE A CROCHET STANDARD THAT CAN BE ENDLESSLY VARIED, JUST BY CHANGING THE COLORS. SQUARES CAN BE COMBINED FOR LARGE AND SMALL GARMENTS, PARTS OF GARMENTS, THROWS, BED COVERS, TABLE RUNNERS, AND SO MUCH MORE.

Yarn: Falk from Dale Garn (CYCA #2 [sport/baby], 100% wool, 116 yd/106 m / 50 g). We used 10 different colors of leftover yarns. Choose the colors to match your interior.

Crochet Hook: U.S. size D-3 or E-4 / 3 or 3.5 mm

Finished Measurements: 35½ x 35½ in / 90 x 90 cm

25 large squares, 96 small squares

Large square: Work 6 rounds

Small square: Work 3 rounds

NOTE: When changing colors, use the next color of yarn to work the slip stitch joining previous round.

Ch 6 and join into a ring with 1 sl st to 1st ch.

Rnd 1: Ch 3, 2 dc around ring, (ch 3, 3 dc around ring) 3 times, ch 3. End with 1 sl st into top of ch 3 at beg of rnd.

Rnd 2: Ch 3, 2 dc in same space (= corner), *ch 1, (3 dc, ch 3, 3 dc) in next space; rep from * 2 more times, ch 1. End with 3 dc, ch 3 in corner and 1 sl st into top of ch 3 at beg of rnd.

Rnd 3: Ch 3, 2 dc in same space (corner), *ch 1, 3 dc in ch-1 loop, ch 1, (3 dc, ch 3, 3 dc) in next ch-3 loop; rep from * 2 more times, ch 1. End with 3 dc in ch-1 loop, ch 1, 3 dc in last corner, ch 3, and 1 sl st into top of ch 3 at beg of rnd.

Rnd 4: Ch 3, 2 dc in same space (corner), *(ch 1, 3 dc in ch-1 loop) 2 times, ch 1, (3 dc, ch 3, 3 dc)

in next ch-3 loop; rep from * 2 more times, (ch 1, 3 dc in ch-1 loop) 2 times, ch 1. End with 3 dc in last corner, ch 3, and 1 sl st into top of ch 3 at beg of rnd.

Continue as set, with 1 more 3-dc group along each long side in each round, until the square is desired side.

Finishing

Join 4 x 4 small squares into a large block, making a total of 24 blocks. The coverlet consists of 7 x 7 large blocks = 49 blocks total.

Cozy coverlet

Blanket with Sunflowers

THIS BLANKET WAS INSPIRED BY A PATTERN WE FOUND IN AN OLD WEEKLY MAGAZINE. ORIGINALLY THE DESIGN WAS WORKED AS A PILLOW COVER. WE DECIDED TO PLAY WITH SOME COLOR CHANGES TO PRODUCE A SUNFLOWER EFFECT.

Yarn: Merino Extra Fine from Drops (CYCA #3 [DK/light worsted], 100% Merino wool, 115 yd/105 m / 50 g)

Yarn Amounts:

150 g Color 1: Mustard
200 g Color 2: Natural White
250 g Color 3: Light Gray-Green
250 g Color 4: North Sea
400 g Color 5: Light Gray

Crochet Hook: U.S. size 7 / 4.5 mm for crocheting squares; U.S. size 4 / 3.5 mm for joining squares

Finished Measurements: 5 x 7 squares = 35½ x 51¼ in / 90 x 130 cm

Each square measures approx. 7 x 7 in / 18 x 18 cm

2 tr group (2 tr gr): (Work 1 tr but do not work last step of bringing yarn through last 2 loops) 2 times into the same st = 3 loops rem on hook. Yoh and through all 3 rem loops.

5 tr group (5 tr gr): (Work 1 tr but do not work last step of bringing yarn through last 2 loops) 5 times into the same st = 6 loops rem on hook. Yoh and through all 6 rem loops.

Tip

To avoid having to weave in all the ends at the end, try this method: Lay the strand you had previously crocheted with next to the new color along the top of the previous row. Work 5-7 sts over both strands. Now complete the rnd as usual. For more details, see page 152 in the Crochet School section.

With Color 1 and larger crochet hook, ch 5 and join into a ring with 1 sl st into 1st ch.

Rnd 1: Ch 3 (= 1st dc), work 15 dc around ring = 16 dc; end with 1 sl st into ch 3 at beg of rnd.

Rnd 2: Ch 4 (= 1 tr), 1 tr in next st, yoh and through ch and treble (= 2 tr gr), (ch 2, 2 tr gr in next st) around. Change to Color 2 and make 1 sl st into top of ch 4 at beg of rnd = 16 2 tr groups.

Rnd 3: Ch 4 (= 1 tr), 4 tr gr worked in, respectively, the next ch loop (3 trebles) and in the top of the next tr group, ch 3, (5 tr gr into next tr working 1st tr into next tr and then 3 tr around ch loop, and 1 tr in next tr, ch 3) around. Change to Color 3 and make 1 sl st into top of ch 4 at beg of rnd.

»——→

Rnd 4: Ch 4 (= 1 tr), 3 tr in ch loop, *(4 tr in next ch loop) 4 times, ch 1, 4 tr in same ch loop (= corner); rep from * around, ending with 4 tr in 1st ch loop, ch 1. Change to Color 4 and make 1 sl st into top of ch 4 at beg of rnd.

Rnd 5: Ch 4 (= 1 tr), 3 tr in ch loop (= corner), 4 tr in next ch loop (between the 4 tr), 4 more times, ch 1, 4 tr in same ch loop (= corner), *(4 tr in next ch loop) 5 times, ch 1, 4 tr in same ch loop (= corner); rep from * around, ending with 4 tr in 1st ch loop. Change to Color 5 and make 1 sl st into top of ch 4 at beg of rnd.

Rnd 6: Ch 4 (= 1 tr), 3 tr in ch loop (= corner), 4 tr in next ch loop (between the 4 tr), 5 more times, ch 1, 4 tr in same ch loop (= corner), *(4 tr in next ch loop) 6 times, ch 1, 4 tr in same ch loop (= corner); rep from * around, ending with 4 tr in 1st ch loop, 1 sl st into top of ch 4 at beg of rnd.

Finishing

With smaller hook, join 5 squares across as follows: Place 2 squares next to each other with RS facing out. Work sc between both squares in each stitch along one side. Join each additional square until 5 squares have been joined. Make a total of 7 strips of squares. Join the strips.

LACE EDGING

With larger hook and Color 5, begin 4 sts before a corner and work a lace edging all the way around the blanket as follows: (1 sc, skip 2 sts, work 5 dc in next st, skip 2 sts) around and end with 1 sl st into 1st sc.

NOTE: Since the stitch count for the lace edging might not work evenly into the stitch count around the edge of the blanket, you may need to adjust the pattern slightly as you go around.

Lace Baby Blanket

WHETHER IT IS USED AS A CHRISTENING GIFT OR A THROW, THIS BLANKET IS EASY TO CROCHET. MAYBE YOU'D LIKE TO EMBELLISH IT WITH A FEW FLOWERS?

Yarn: Baby Ull from Dale Garn (CYCA #1, 100% wool, 180 yd/165 m / 50 g)
Yarn Amounts:
350 g White
Crochet Hook: U.S. size D-3 / 3 mm
Gauge: approx. 5 dc gr = 4 in / 10 cm. Adjust hook size to obtain correct gauge if necessary.
Measurements: Width, approx. 31½ in / 80 cm; length approx. 39½ in / 100 cm at widest point

The pattern is a multiple of 5 sts + 5 sts for the foundation chain.

Loosely ch 175.

Row 1: Beginning in 6th ch from hook, work the first dc group (= dc gr): *(2 dc, ch 1, 2 dc) in same st, skip 2 ch*; rep * to * across, ending with 1 dc in last ch.
Row 2: Ch 3 (= 1st dc), *(2 dc, ch 1, 2 dc) in next ch-1 loop; rep from * across, ending with 1 dc in last dc.
Repeat Row 2 until blanket is desired length.

Edging: Work dc groups all around the edges of the blanket. If desired, work the edging in a contrast color suitable for the baby.
Finishing: Weave in all ends. Gently wash blanket, following instructions on yarn ball band. Lay blanket flat to dry, patted out to finished measurements. The blanket will stretch slightly so take that into consideration when blocking blanket.

Lace baby blanket

Chevron Blanket

THE CHEVRON PATTERN HAS ALWAYS GENERATED A LOT OF INTEREST. THERE ARE ENDLESS WAYS TO VARY IT—THE STRIPES CAN BE STEEP OR GENTLE, WIDE OR NARROW, ALIKE OR DIFFERENT.

Yarn: Karisma from Drops (CYCA #3 [DK/light worsted], 100% Merino wool, 109 yd/100 m / 50 g)

Yarn Amounts:
300 g **Color 1:** Beige Heather
200 g **Color 2:** Chocolate Brown
150 g **Color 3:** Cerise
100 g **Color 4:** Lavender/Gray Lilac
100 g **Color 5:** Natural White
100 g **Color 6:** Dark Old Rose
100 g **Color 7:** Light Turquoise
Crochet Hook: U.S. size J-10 / 6 mm
Finished Measurements: approx. 59 in / 150 cm long

Fasten off ends at every color change—see pages 152 and 161 in the Crochet School section.

With Color 1, ch 194.

Row 1: Work 1 dc in 4th ch from hook, 1 dc in each of the next 12 ch, (skip 4 ch, 1 dc in each of next 14 ch, ch 3, 1 dc in each of next 14 ch) 5 times, skip 4 ch, 1 dc in each of the last 14 ch = 168 dc.

Row 2: Ch 3 (= 1st dc), 1 dc in first dc, 2 dc in next dc, 1 dc in each of the next 10 dc, *skip 4 dc, 1 dc in each of next 12 dc, (2 dc in ch loop, ch 3, 2 dc) in same ch loop, 1 dc in each of next 12 dc; rep from * 4 more times, skip 4 dc. End with 1 dc in each of next 10 dc, 2 dc in each of the last 2 dc = 168 dc.

Rows 3–5: Change to Color 2 and work as for Row 2.

Row 6: Change to Color 6 and work as for Row 2.

Rows 7–8: Change to Color 1 and work as for Row 2.

Row 9: Change to Color 5 and work as for Row 2.

Row 10: Change to Color 1 and work as for Row 2.

Row 11: Change to Color 2 and work as for Row 2.

Rows 12–15: Change to Color 1 and work as for Row 2.

Row 16: Change to Color 4 and work as for Row 2.

Row 17: Change to Color 6 and work as for Row 2.

Rows 18–20: Change to Color 3 and work as for Row 2.

Row 21: Change to Color 6 and work as for Row 2.

Rows 22–23: Change to Color 1 and work as for Row 2.

Rows 24–25: Change to Color 5 and work as for Row 2.

Rows 26–29: Change to Color 4 and work as for Row 2.

Row 30: Change to Color 2 and work as for Row 2.

Chevron blanket

Row 31: Change to Color 7 and work as for Row 2.

Rows 32–34: Change to Color 1 and work as for Row 2.

Row 35: Change to Color 3 and work as for Row 2.

Row 36: Change to Color 5 and work as for Row 2.

Rows 37–40: Change to Color 7 and work as for Row 2.

Row 41: Change to Color 1 and work as for Row 2.

Rows 42–43: Change to Color 2 and work as for Row 2.

Row 44: Change to Color 4 and work as for Row 2.

Rows 45–47: Change to Color 3 and work as for Row 2.

Rows 48–49: Change to Color 1 and work as for Row 2.

Rows 50–51: Change to Color 6 and work as for Row 2.

Rows 52–55: Change to Color 2 and work as for Row 2.

Row 56: Change to Color 7 and work as for Row 2.

Rows 57–58: Change to Color 4 and work as for Row 2.

Row 59: Change to Color 5 and work as for Row 2.

Rows 60–61: Change to Color 1 and work as for Row 2.

Row 62: Change to Color 6 and work as for Row 2.

Rows 63–65: Change to Color 3 and work as for Row 2.

Row 66: Change to Color 6 and work as for Row 2.

Row 67: Change to Color 4 and work as for Row 2.

Rows 68–71: Change to Color 1 and work as for Row 2.

Row 72: Change to Color 2 and work as for Row 2.

Row 73: Change to Color 1 and work as for Row 2.

Row 74: Change to Color 5 and work as for Row 2.

Rows 75–76: Change to Color 1 and work as for Row 2.

Row 77: Change to Color 6 and work as for Row 2.

Rows 78–80: Change to Color 2 and work as for Row 2.

Rows 81–82: Change to Color 1 and work as for Row 2.

Weave in all ends neatly on WS.

Tip
If you want a blanket with less steep chevrons, half the number of stitches (from 12 to 6 sts) between decreases and increases across the row.

Sweet Pillows with
Traditional Crochet Edgings

WE FOUND THESE EDGINGS IN AN OLD WORKBOOK OF CROCHET DESIGNS FROM THE 1950S. THE EDGINGS WILL LOOK VERY NICE AT THE LOWER EDGE OF A GARMENT, BLANKET, OR AROUND A HANDKERCHIEF. THE THIRD EDGING CONSISTS OF LOOPS AND CAN BE CROCHETED AS LONG AS YOU LIKE BECAUSE IT GROWS LENGTHWISE. WE USED ALL THREE EDGINGS FOR PILLOW COVERS.

All the edgings are approx. 2¼ yd / 2 m long, which will fit around a pillow 19¾ x 19¾ in / 50 x 50 cm.

Edging 1

Yarn: Mandarin Petit from SandnesGarn (CYCA #1 [sock/fingering/baby], 100% cotton, 195 yd/178 m / 50 g), approx. 50 g Red
Crochet Hook: U.S. size D-3 / 3 mm
Measurements: approx. 2 in / 5 cm wide

Pattern Stitch:
3 tr group (3 tr gr): (Work 1 tr but do not work last step of bringing yarn through last 2 loops) 3 times into the same st = 4 loops rem on hook. Yoh and through all 4 rem loops.

Chain enough stitches to make a strip long enough to go across/around the item to be edged. The stitch count should be a multiple of 5 + 2 sts.

Row 1: Work 1 tr, 2 tr gr in the 5th ch from the hook (= 1 tr group), (ch 6, 1 tr gr in the same st, skip 4 sts, 1 tr gr in next st) across, ending with ch 6, 1 tr gr in same st; turn.

Row 2: Ch 4 (= 1st tr), 2 tr gr in the ch-6 loop of previous row, (ch 6, 3 tr gr in same ch loop, 3 tr gr in next ch loop) across, ending with ch 6, 3 tr gr in last ch loop.

Row 3: Begin with 1 sl st in the first 6 ch loop of previous row. Continue with [ch 3 (= 1st dc), 3 dc, ch 4, 4 dc] in ch-6 loop. *(3 sc, ch 3, 3 sc) in next ch loop, (4 dc, ch 4, 4 dc) in next loop; rep from * across.
Cut thread and fasten off.

Edging 2

Yarn: Mandarin Petit from SandnesGarn (CYCA #1 [sock/fingering/baby], 100% cotton, 195 yd/178 m / 50 g), approx. 100 g Peach
Crochet Hook: U.S. size C-2–D-3 / 2.5–3 mm
Measurements: approx. 1½ in / 4 cm wide

Pattern Stitch:
Work tr groups as described for Edging 1 but this time with the hook inserted into the new sc for each dc.

Chain enough stitches to make a strip long enough to go across/around the item to be

»⟶

Sweet pillows with traditional crochet edgings

edged. The stitch count should be a multiple of 5 + 2 sts.

Row 1: Beginning in 2nd ch from hook, work sc across; turn.

Row 2: Ch 4 (= 1st tr), 2 tr gr in the next 2 sc, *ch 3, 1 tr, skip 1 sc, 3 tr gr in next 3 sc; continue from * across; turn.

Row 3: *2 tr gr, ch 3, 2 tr gr, ch 3, 2 tr gr in next ch-3 loop, 1 sc before the next ch loop; rep from * across; turn.

Row 4: 1 sl st in 1st tr gr of previous row, 1 sc in same tr gr. (3 sc in ch loop, 1 sc above tr gr, 4 sc in next ch loop, 1 sc above tr gr) across. Cut thread and weave in all ends neatly on WS.

Edging 3

Yarn: Pt Pandora from Rauma (CYCA #1 [sock/fingering/baby], 100% cotton, 180 yd/165 m / 50 g) approx. 50 g Green
Crochet Hook: U.S. size D-3 / 3 mm
Measurements: approx. 2 in / 5 cm wide

Ch 11 and join into a ring with 1 sl st into 1st ch.

Loop 1: Ch 3 (= 1st dc), work 9 dc around ring = 10 dc.

Loop 2 and following: *Ch 11, 1 sc in last worked dc, ch 1, 1 sc in same ring as dc; turn. Work 10 dc in the last of ch-11 ring; rep from * to desired length.

BORDER

Row 1: Ch 6, (3 tr in ch directly above the 10 dc, ch 5, 1 sc in 5th dc, ch 5) across, ending with 3 tr, ch 6, 1 sc above outermost dc.

Row 2: Turn with ch 1, 3 sc in first ch loop, ch 4, skip 3 tr, (3 sc in next ch loop, ch 5) across, ending with 3 sc in last ch loop.

Row 3: Turn with ch 3, work 1 dc in each sc and 5 dc in each ch loop. End with 1 dc at outer edge.

Finishing
Hand- or machine-stitch the edging around a pillow cover. If necessary, sew in a zipper for closure.

Sweet pillows with traditional crochet edgings

Pillows

WHILE THE CHAIR CUSHION IS MADE WITH A HARMONIOUS RANGE OF BLUE/TURQUOISE/LILAC SHADES, THE PILLOW COVER IS CROCHETED WITH ALL THE COLORS OF THE RAINBOW. FEEL FREE TO CHOOSE YOUR OWN COLOR SCHEME.

Yarn: Pt Petunia from Rauma (CYCA #3 [DK/light worsted], 100% cotton, 120 yd/110 m / 50 g)

Yarn Amounts:

Pillow 1 in rainbow colors	*Pillow 2 in blue/ turquoise/lilac*
1 ball each of:	**1 ball each of:**
Color 1: Turquoise	**Color 1:** Dark Lilac
Color 2: Light Pink	**Color 2:** Dark Turquoise
Color 3: Light Green	**Color 3:** Lime
Color 4: Red	**Color 4:** Sea-Green
Color 5: Blue	**Color 5:** Light Turquoise
Color 6: Orange	**Color 6:** Medium Lilac
Color 7: Blue-Green	**Color 7:** Blue

Crochet Hook: U.S. size E-4 / 3.5 mm

Measurements: The pillow cover is approx. 17¾ in / 45 cm in diameter (or to fit pillow)

NOTE: Change colors on every round. All rounds begin with ch 3 (= 1st dc) and end with 1 sl st into the top of ch 3 at beg of rnd.

RAINBOW PILLOW

With Color 1, ch 6 and join into a ring with 1 sl st into 1st ch.

Rnd 1: Ch 3, work 11 dc around ring = 12 dc; end with 1 sl st into top of ch 3 at beg of rnd.

Rnd 2: Ch 3 (= 1st dc), work 2 dc in each dc around = 24 dc; end with 1 sl st into top of ch 3 at beg of rnd.

Rnd 3: Change to Color 2. Ch 3 (= 1st dc), (1 dc in next st, 2 dc in next st) = 36 dc; end with 1 sl st into top of ch 3 at beg of rnd.

Rnd 4: Change to Color 3. Ch 3 (= 1st dc), (1 dc in each of next 2 sts, 2 dc in next st) = 48 dc; end with 1 sl st into top of ch 3 at beg of rnd.

Rnd 5: Change to Color 4. Ch 3 (= 1st dc), (1 dc in each of next 3 sts, 2 dc in next st) = 60 dc; end with 1 sl st into top of ch 3 at beg of rnd.

Rnd 6: Change to Color 5. Ch 3 (= 1st dc), (1 dc in each of next 4 sts, 2 dc in next st) = 72 dc; end with 1 sl st into top of ch 3 at beg of rnd.

Rnd 7: Change to Color 6. Ch 3 (= 1st dc), (1 dc in each of next 5 sts, 2 dc in next st) = 84 dc; end with 1 sl st into top of ch 3 at beg of rnd.

Rnd 8: Change to Color 7. Ch 3 (= 1st dc), (1 dc in each of next 6 sts, 2 dc in next st) = 96 dc; end with 1 sl st into top of ch 3 at beg of rnd.

Continue in this same color sequence (or as you like) and work 1 dc more between each increase on each rnd: Color 1, Color 3, Color 2, Color 5, Color 6, Color 7, Color 4, Color 6, Color 5, Color 2, Color 1.

PILLOW IN SHADES OF BLUE/TURQUOISE/LILAC

Work as for Rainbow Pillow.

Rose Potholder

THIS METHOD OF CROCHETING A ROSE MOTIF WAS USED VERY FRE-
QUENTLY IN THE 1940S. SINCE THE BACKING WAS FLAT, IT COULD
BE USED FOR SO MANY ITEMS—POTHOLDERS, EMBELLISHMENTS FOR
SWEATERS AND JACKETS, POCKETS, OR THE FRONT OF A VEST. YOU CAN
MAKE THE MOTIF IN ONE OR SEVERAL COLORS. IF YOU HAVE A STASH
OF COTTON YARN, THIS IS A GREAT PROJECT FOR USING SOME UP!

Yarn: Paris from Drops (CYCA #4 [worsted/af-
ghan/aran], 100% cotton, 82 yd/75 m / 50 g),
50 g each of
Color 1: Light Mint Green
Color 2: Dusty Rose
Color 3: Medium Pink
Color 4: Light Peach
Color 5: Dark Old Rose
Crochet Hook: U.S. size 7 / 4.5 mm
Measurements: The flower measures approx.
8¾ in / 22 cm in diameter; add more rounds if
you want a wider potholder.

Pattern:
The firm backing is achieved by crocheting
alternately through the front and back stitch
loops as indicated in the instructions. The
petals are worked over 5 sts. You will increase
15 sts on every 4th rnd until the potholder is
desired size.

With Color 1, ch 6 and join into a ring with 1 sl
st into 1st ch.

Rnd 1: Ch 1 (= 1st sc), 14 sc around ring = 15 sc.

Rnd 2: Ch 3 (= 1st dc), 1 dc in next st, work 2 dc
in each st around = 30 dc; end with 1 sl st into
top of ch 3 at beg of rnd.

Rnd 3: Change to Color 2. Work sts on this rnd
by inserting the hook through the front loop of
the stitch on previous rnd. Begin with ch 1 (= 1st
sc). 1 hdc in next st, 5 dc in next st, 1 hdc in next
st, 1 sc in next st (= 1st rose petal worked over 5
sts). Continue with (1 sc, 1 hdc, 5 st in same st, 1
hdc, 1 sc) around; end with 1 sl st into 1st ch = 6
rose petals.

Rnd 4: Work sts on this rnd by inserting the
hook through the back loops on sts from Rnd 2
(Color 1). With the front of the work facing you,
crochet into the back. Begin with 1 sl st and
then ch 3 (= 1st dc), 1 dc in st from Rnd 2, 1 dc in
next st, (2 dc in next st, 1 dc in next st) around,
ending with 1 sl st into top of ch 3 at beg of rnd
= 45 dc.

Rnd 5: Change to Color 3. Work sts on this rnd
by inserting the hook through the front loop of
the stitch on previous rnd. Begin with ch 1 (= 1st
sc). 1 sc in next st, 1 hdc, 5 dc in same st, 1 hdc,
1 sc in next st. Continue as for Rnd 3 = 9 petals.

Rnd 6: Work sts on this rnd by inserting the
hook through the back loop on st from Rnd 4.
Begin with 1 sl st and then ch 3 (= 1st dc), 1 dc
in st from Rnd 4, (1 dc in next st) around = 45
dc—no increases. End with 1 sl st into top of ch
3 at beg of rnd.

Rnd 7: Change to Color 4. Work as for Rnd 5 =
9 petals.

Rnd 8: Work sts on this rnd by inserting the hook through the back loop on st from Rnd 6. Begin with 1 sl st and then ch 3 (= 1st dc), 1 dc in st from Rnd 6, 1 dc in each of next 2 sts, (2 dc in next st, 1 dc in each of next 2 sts) around, ending with 1 sl st into top of ch 3 at beg of rnd = 60 dc.

Rnd 9: Change to Color 5. Work as for Rnd 5 = 12 petals.

Rnd 10: Work as for Rnd 6, without any increases = 60 dc.

Rnd 11: Change to Color 3. Work as for Rnd 9 = 12 petals.

Rnd 12: Change to Color 1. Work sts on this rnd by inserting the hook through the back loop on st from Rnd 10. Begin with 1 sl st and then ch 3 (= 1st dc), 1 dc in st from Rnd 10, 1 dc in each of next 3 sts, (2 dc in next st, 1 dc in each of next 3 sts) around, ending with 1 sl st into top of ch 3 at beg of rnd = 75 dc.

Rnd 13: Work as for Rnd 5 = 15 petals.

Cut yarn and weave in all ends neatly on WS.

RING AT CENTER (Color 4)
Hold the yarn on the back of the piece. Insert the hook through from the RS and pull up a loop. Insert the hook 1 st forward and pull up a new loop. Continue the same way until you've crocheted a circle. Cut yarn and weave in end on WS.

HANGING LOOP
With Color 1, attach yarn between two petals and ch 20-25; turn and sc back. Cut yarn and weave ends on WS.

Rose potholder

Multi-Color Potholder

A THICK AND PRACTICAL POTHOLDER
TO LIVEN UP YOUR KITCHEN! SPEEDY
CROCHETING! CHOOSE COLORS TO MATCH
YOUR KITCHEN. FOR A DECORATIVE VERSION,
WE EVEN USED A BIT OF GLITTER THREAD.

Yarn: Heavy cotton yarn, 50 g of each of 5 colors + a little glitter thread (optional)
Crochet Hook: U.S. size G-6 / 4 mm
Measurements: 8 x 8 in / 20 x 20 cm

Tip
Change colors by working the last step of the last stitch on the previous row with the new color. For some rows, we held glitter thread together with the cotton yarn. Always work the last st of the row with a dc in the top of the ch 3 from previous row.

Hanging Loop and Row 1: With any color, ch 14 and join into a ring with 1 sl st into 1st ch. Ch 1, work 18 sc around ring, 3 dc, ch 2, 3 dc around ring; turn.

Row 2: Ch 3 (= 1st dc), 2 dc, (2 dc, ch 2, 2 dc) in ch loop, 3 dc. Change colors.

Row 3: Ch 3 (= 1st dc), 4 dc, (2 dc, ch 2, 2 dc) in ch loop, 5 dc. Change colors.

Row 4: Ch 3 (= 1st dc), 6 dc, (2 dc, ch 2, 2 dc) in ch loop, 7 dc. Change colors.

Row 5: Ch 3 (= 1st dc), 8 dc, (2 dc, ch 2, 2 dc) in ch loop, 9 dc. Change colors.

Rows 6–15: Continue as set, with 2 more dc on each side of ch loop on every row.

Cut yarn and weave in ends neatly on WS.

Star Motif Potholder

THIS POTHOLDER IS A CLASSIC! IT WAS CROCHETED IN COLORS TO MATCH CURTAINS AND OTHER FURNISHINGS. THE CENTER IS DOUBLED AND OFFERS GOOD INSULATION. THIS VERSION IS CROCHETED IN HEAVIER YARN SO YOU WILL HAVE A GOOD-SIZED POTHOLDER.

Yarn: Paris from Drops (CYCA #4 [worsted/afghan/aran], 100% cotton, 82 yd/75 m / 50 g), 50 g each of:

Color 1: Natural White
Color 2: Light Orange
Color 3: Medium Lilac
Color 4: Bright Yellow
Crochet Hook: U.S. size 7 / 4.5 mm
Measurements: The potholder measures approx. 9¾ in / 25 cm in diameter

CENTER SECTION

With Color 1, ch 6 and join into a ring with 1 sl st into 1st ch.

Rnd 1: (Ch 5, 1 sc around ring) 6 times = 6 ch loops.

Rnd 2: 1 sl st into 1st ch loop, ch 3 (= 1st dc), 4 dc around ch loop. Work 5 dc around each ch loop around = 30 dc. End with 1 sl st into top of ch 3 at beg of rnd.

Rnd 3: Ch 3 (= 1st dc), 4 dc, (5 dc through back loops—see page 155, ch 3) around, ending with 1 sl st into to of ch 3 at beg of rnd.

Rnd 4: 1 sl st into backmost ch loop of 1 dc, ch 5, 2 yarnovers around hook, insert hook through the back loop of next dc and bring up 1 loop, bring yarn through 2 loops 2 times, 1 yoh, bring up 1 loop, bring yarn through 2 loops 1 time, 1 yoh, bring up 1 loop (= 5 loops on hook), bring through 2 loops at a time 4 times, (ch 10, 1 sc into front of next dc group, ch 10, 2 yarnovers around hook, insert hook through back stitch loop of next dc and bring up 1 loop, yarn through 2 loops 2 times, 2 yarnovers around hook, bring up 1 loop, yarn through 2 loops 2 times, 1 yoh, bring up 1 loop, bring through 2 loops 1 time, 1 yoh, bring up 1 loop (= 6 loops on hook), bring through 2 loops at a time 5 times) around. End with ch 10, 1 sc, ch 10, 1 sl st into top of 1st point (= 6 points and 12 ch loops).

Rnd 5: Sl st to top of 1st ch loop, (ch 7, 1 sc in top of next ch loop) around, ending with 1 sl st into 1st loop at beg of rnd.

BACK

Ch 5 and join into a ring with 1 sl st into 1st ch. Begin each rnd with ch 1 (= 1st sc) and end with 1 sl st into 1st st.

Rnd 1: Work 8 sc around ring.

Rnd 2: Work 2 sc in each sc around = 16 sc.

»——→

Rnd 3: Work 1 sc in next st, 2 sc in next st = 24 sc.

Rnd 4: Work 1 sc in each of next 2 sts, 2 sc in next st = 32 sc.

Rnd 5: Work 1 sc in each of next 3 sts, 2 sc in next st = 40 sc.

Rnd 6: Work 1 sc in each of next 4 sts, 2 sc in next st = 48 sc.

Rnd 7: Work 1 sc in each of next 5 sts, 2 sc in next st = 56 sc.

Rnds 8–12: Continue in sc, with 1 more sc between each increase, until there are a total of 96 sc.

JOINING

Place the pieces together with the center section on top.

Rnd 1 (Color 3): 1 sl st into 1st ch loop, ch 3 (= 1st dc), 5 dc around ch loop, (ch 4, skip 2 sc, 6 dc around next ch loop) around, ending with ch 4, 1 sl st into top of ch 3 at beg of rnd.

Rnd 2 (Color 1): Ch 3 (= 1st dc), 3 dc around ch loop, *(4 dc, ch 4, 4 dc) around next ch loop; rep from * around, ending with 4 dc, ch 4, 1 sl st into top of ch 3 at beg of rnd. Sl st over the 1st dc group.

Rnd 3 (Color 4): 1 sl st at center of dc group of previous rnd, (12 hdc around ch loop, 1 sc at center of dc group) around, ending with 1 sl st into 1st st.

Rnd 4 (Color 1): Work a picot edging through back loops of stitches around: (1 sc, ch 3, 1 sc in the 1st of the 3 ch, 1 sc) around.

HANGING LOOP

With Color 3, ch 20-25; turn and, beginning in 2nd ch from hook, sc back; attach to potholder with 1 sl st.

Weave in all ends neatly on WS.

Flower Potholders

A PRETTY AND PRACTICAL OLD-FASHIONED POTHOLDER IN FRESH COLORS. THE PETALS ARE CROCHETED FIRST, WITH THE HANGING LOOP AND PETAL SURROUNDS AS THE FINISHING TOUCHES.

Yarn: Pt Petunia from Rauma (CYCA #3 [DK/light worsted], 100% cotton, 120 yd/110 m / 50 g)

Yarn Amounts: 50 g of each color

Red version	*Blue version*
Color 1: Gray	**Color 1:** Gray
Color 2: Yellow	**Color 2:** Light Green
Color 3: Light Pink	**Color 3:** Lime
Color 4: Deep Pink	**Color 4:** Turquoise
Color 5: Lacquer Red	**Color 5:** Green
Color 6: Red	**Color 6:** Blue

Crochet Hook: U.S. size D-3 or E-4 / 3 or 3.5 mm

Measurements: approx. 9¾ in / 25 cm in diameter

The color changes at the end of every other rnd with a sl st in the new color.

With Color 1, ch 5 and join into a ring with 1 sl st into 1st st.

»——→

Flower potholders

Rnd 1: Ch 3 (= 1st dc), work 14 dc around ring = 15 dc; end with 1 sl st into top of ch 3 at beg of rnd.

Rnd 2: Ch 3 (= 1st dc) and work 2 dc into each st around = 30 dc. Change color with 1 sl st into top of ch 3 at beg of rnd.

Rnd 3: Ch 4 (= 1st dc + 1 ch), *skip next dc, (1 dc, ch 1, 1 dc) in next dc; rep from * around. End with 1 dc in sl st of previous rnd, ch 1, 1 sl st into 3rd ch at beg of rnd. You should now have 15 Vs with a ch 1 between each V.

Rnd 4: Ch 4 (= 1st dc + 1 ch), skip to center of 1st V, work *(1 dc, ch 1, 1 dc), ch 1, skip to center of next V; rep from * around, ending with 1 dc, ch 1; change colors with 1 sl st into 3rd ch at beg of rnd.

Rnd 5: Ch 4 (= 1st dc + 1 ch), skip to center of 1st V, work *(2 dc, ch 1, 2 dc), ch 1, skip to center of next V; rep from * around, ending with 2 dc, ch 1, 1 dc, 1 sl st into 3rd ch at beg of rnd.

Rnd 6: Work as for Rnd 5. Change colors at end of rnd.

Rnd 7: Ch 4 (= 1st dc + 1 ch), skip to center of 1st V, work *(3 dc, ch 1, 3 dc), ch 1, skip to center of next V; rep from * around, ending with 3 dc, ch 1, 2 dc, 1 sl st into 3rd ch at beg of rnd.

Rnd 8: Work as for Rnd 7. Change colors at end of rnd.

Rnd 9: Ch 4 (= 1st dc + 1 ch), skip to center of 1st V, work *(4 dc, ch 1, 4 dc), ch 1, skip to center of next V; rep from * around, ending with 4 dc, ch 1, 3 dc, 1 sl st into 3rd ch at beg of rnd.

Rnd 10: Work as for Rnd 9. Change colors at end of rnd.

Rnd 11: Ch 4 (= 1st dc + 1 ch), skip to center of 1st V, *work 11 dc in a V, ch 1, skip to center of next V; rep from *. In the last V, work 10 dc and end with 1 sl st into 3rd ch at beg of rnd.

HANGING LOOP AND FINISHING

Ch 20-25 and join into a ring with 1 sl st into 1st ch. Sc around ring. Join the loop at the top of the potholder between the first and last petal of the round with 1 sc, ch 2. Continue in sc down between the petals, with 1 sc in each ch loop (chain loops in this context are the chain stitches worked on each side of the Vs) + ch 2 in each space down to the 2nd rnd. Turn and sc back up the same way. Work 1 sc in each stitch around the top of the petal. Continue down, up, and around each petal until you are back at the starting point. Attach last sc to the other side of the hanging loop with a sl st.

Weave in all ends neatly on WS.

Flower potholders

Grill Mitt

HERE'S THE PERFECT GRILL MITT FOR YOUR NEXT SUMMER COOKOUT.

Yarn: Paris from Drops (CYCA #4 [worsted/afghan/aran], 100% cotton, 82 yd/75 m / 50 g), 50 g each of:
Color 1: Denim
Color 2: Light Gray
Color 3: Light Mint Green

Crochet Hook: U.S. size E-4 or G-6 / 3.5 or 4 mm
Measurements: Total length 12¼ in / 31 cm

The grill mitt is crocheted from the bottom up and consists of two pieces that are crocheted

together. It is worked in single crochet with 2 rows of each color in the following color sequence throughout: Color 1, Color 2, Color 3.

Ch 23.

Row 1: Beg in 3rd ch from hook, sc across.

Row 2: Ch 1 (= 1st sc), work in sc across = 22 sc.

Rows 3–7: Work as for Row 2, changing colors in sequence. Subsequent rows without any increases or decreases are worked the same way. After increasing/decreasing at beginning or end of row as specified, work 1 sc in each of all other sts across.

Row 8: Increase 1 sc (work 2 sc into 1 st) at beg of row = 23 sc.

Row 12: Increase 1 sc (work 2 sc into 1 st) at beg of row = 24 sc.

Row 16: Increase 1 sc (work 2 sc into 1 st) at beg of row = 25 sc.

Row 20: Increase 1 sc (work 2 sc into 1 st) at beg of row = 26 sc.

Row 22: Increase 1 sc (work 2 sc into 1 st) at beg of row = 27 sc.

Row 24: Increase 1 sc (work 2 sc into 1 st) at beg of row = 28 sc.

Row 26: Increase 1 sc (work 2 sc into 1 st) at beg of row = 29 sc.

Row 28: Increase 1 sc (work 2 sc into 1 st) at beg of row = 30 sc.

Row 30: Increase 1 sc (work 2 sc into 1 st) at beg of row = 31 sc.

Row 31: Work 21 sc; turn. The 10 sts left unworked will be used later for the thumb.

Row 32: Decrease 1 st at end of row (see page 150 in the Crochet School section). 20 sc rem.

Row 43: Decrease 1 st each at beg and end of row = 18 sc rem.

Row 47: Decrease 1 st each at beg and end of row = 16 sc rem.

Row 49: Decrease 1 st each at beg and end of row = 14 sc rem.

Row 51: Decrease 1 st each at beg and end of row = 12 sc rem.

Row 52: Decrease 1 st each at beg and end of row = 10 sc rem. Cut yarn and fasten off.

THUMB

Row 1: Attach yarn (using correct color in sequence) 1 st over from the split on Row 31 and sc across = 9 sc.

Row 2: Increase 1 st at beg of row = 10 sc.

Row 3: Work 10 sc across.

Row 4: Increase 1 st at beg of row = 11 sc.

Row 5: Decrease 1 st at beg of row = 10 sc rem.

Row 6: Work 10 sc across.

Row 7: Decrease 1 st at beg of row = 9 sc rem.

Row 8: Decrease 1 st at beg of row = 8 sc rem.

Row 9: Decrease 1 st at beg of row = 7 sc rem.

Row 10: Decrease 1 st each at beg and end of row = 5 sc rem. Cut yarn and fasten off.

Finishing
Weave in all ends on WS. Crochet the pieces together with Color 3 and sc. Change to Color 1 and work back in crab stitch (see Edging 4 on page 141). End by making a hanging loop: With Color 1, ch 25 and then work 24 sc around loop. Attach end to mitt with 1 sl st; cut yarn and fasten off.

Tip
To make the mitt roomier at the cuff, begin with, for example, ch 26 and work 25 sc across through Row 19. Continue as above from Row 20 on.

Grill mitt

Lampshade Cover

MAKE YOUR OWN LAMPSHADES AS THEY DID IN THE GOOD OLD DAYS. YOU CAN CROCHET YOUR OWN DOILIES OR BUY SOME AT A FLEA MARKET OR SECOND HAND SHOP. IT'S NOT A SIN IF YOU USE THE OLD DOILIES FROM YOUR GRANDMOTHER EITHER—THAT JUST MAKES THE SHADE MORE PERSONAL. FOR A WARMER LOOK, DYE WHITE DOILIES IN TEA, MAKING THEM OFF-WHITE.

Materials
Crocheted doilies
Rice paper lampshade, glass lamp globe,
   or round ball
Paste, such as starch
Cord and light bulb

Assembly
Using the rice lampshade or glass globe, arrange the doilies in two stages. Beginning with the top half, use tape and glue to attach the doilies to the ball/globe. Let dry and turn the base over the next day. Attach the rest of the doilies to the bottom half. This method helps because the doilies have a tendency to loosen when they are on the underside of the bottom half of the ball. It will take at least one day for the starch to dry completely. See page 164 for which type of stiffening agent to use. We used carpet glue.

A round ball that can be removed afterwards is an alternative. In that case, the doilies have to be glued on in two steps—one half of the ball at a time. When completely dry, remove the ball and glue the halves together. The lamp consists of only the crocheted doilies.

Angel

THIS ANGEL CAN HANG ON THE CHRISTMAS TREE OR IN A WINDOW. THE PATTERN IS BASED ON AN OLD DESIGN THAT WAS ONCE VERY POPULAR AND MUCH VARIED. ADD YOUR PERSONAL TOUCH TO THE ANGEL BY GIVING IT A BEAD CROWN AROUND THE HEAD OR A CROCHETED HALO IN GOLD THREAD, OR EDGE THE SKIRT WITH GOLD THREAD.

Yarn: Fine cotton yarn, such as Fiol from Solberg Spinderi (CYCA #2 [sport/baby], 100% mercerized cotton, 185 yd/169 m / 50 g), 50 g White or Mandarin Petit from SandnesGarn (CYCA #1 [sock/fingering/baby], 100% cotton, 195 yd/178 m / 50 g), 50 g White
Small amount of leftover yarn for the halo
Crochet Hook: U.S. size A / 2 mm (Fiol) or C-2 / 2.5mm (Mandarin Petit)
Notions: A plastic ring for the halo, or beads

HEAD

Ch 4 and join into a ring with 1 sl st into 1st ch.

NOTE: Work sc through both loops unless otherwise specified.

Rnd 1: Ch 1 (= 1st sc), work 9 sc around ring = 10 sc; end with 1 sl st into 1st ch.

Rnd 2: Ch 1 (= 1st sc), 1 sc in next st, 2 sc in each of rem sts around; end with 1 sl st into 1st ch = 20 sc.

Rnds 3–8: Ch 1 (= 1st sc), 1 sc in each sc around; end with 1 sl st into 1st ch.

Rnd 9: Decrease to 10 sts as follows: Ch 1, insert hook through 1st st, yoh, bring yarn through, insert hook through next st, yoh, bring yarn through; yoh and through the 3 loops on hook. Continue as follows: * Insert hook through next st, yoh, bring yarn through, insert hook through next st, yoh, bring yarn through; yoh and through the 3 loops on hook. Rep from * around and end with 1 sl st into 1st ch = 10 sc.

Rnd 10: Ch 1 (= 1st sc), 1 sc in each sc around; end with 1 sl st into 1st ch.

SHOULDERS

Rnd 11: Ch 5 (= 1 dc + 2 ch), (2 dc in next st, ch 2) around, end with 1 dc, 1 sl st into 3rd ch at beg of rnd = 10 ch loops.

Rnd 12: Ch 3 (= 1st dc), 1 dc in next st, *(ch 3, 1 dc in next ch-2 loop, ch 3), 1 dc in each of next 2 sts; rep from * around, ending with 1 sl st into top of ch 3 at beg of rnd = 20 dc in ch-2 loops.

Tip

If you thread a strand of contrast color yarn through the chain loops, it will be easier to count the number of loops to skip in the following rounds. You can remove the thread once you no longer need it.

BODY

Rnd 13: Ch 3 (= 1st dc), 1 dc in next dc, (ch 1, 1 dc in next ch-3 loop, ch 1, 1 dc in next dc, ch 1, 1 dc in next ch-3 loop, ch 1, 1 dc in each of the next 2 dc, ch 1), skip 8 ch-3 loops, 1 dc in each of the next 2 dc; rep instructions within parenthe-

»——→

ses once. End with skip 8 ch-3 loops, 1 sl st into top of ch 3 at beg of rnd. You will crochet over each wing later on.

Rnd 14: Ch 3 (= 1st dc), 1 dc in next st, (ch 1, 1 dc in each of next 3 sts, ch 1, 1 dc in each of next 2 dc, ch 1), 1 dc in each of the next 2 dc; rep instructions within parentheses once and end with 1 sl st into top of ch 3 at beg of rnd.

Rnd 15: Ch 3, 1 dc in next dc, (ch 2, 2 dc in each of next 3 dc, ch 2, 1 dc in each of next 2 dc, ch 2), 1 dc in each of the next 2 dc; rep instructions within parentheses once and end with 1 sl st into top of ch 3 at beg of rnd.

Rnd 16: Ch 3 (= 1st dc), 1 dc in sl st, ch 1, 2 dc in next dc, ch 2, *2 dc in next dc, ch 1, 2 dc in next dc, ch 2; rep from* around, ending with 1 sl st into top of ch 3 at beg of rnd = 40 dc divided into 10 groups of 4 dc each with 2 ch between each group.

Rnd 17: 1 sl st into 1st ch-1 loop, + ch 3 + 1 dc + ch 1 + 2 dc in same ch-1 loop, ch 2, *2 dc + ch 1, + 2 dc in next ch-1 loop, ch 2; rep from * around. End with 1 sl st into 3rd ch = 10 groups of 4 dc each. The ch-2 between each group should lie directly over the ch-2 loop below.

Rnds 18–20: Work as for Rnd 17.

Rnd 21: 1 sl st in the 1st ch-1 loop, 1 sc in same loop, (3 dc, ch 3, 3 dc) in next ch-2 loop, *1 sc in next ch-1 loop, rep instructions within paren-

theses. Rep from * around, ending with 1 sl st into 1st sc. Cut yarn.

WINGS

Row 1: Attach yarn in the corner below the wing (between 2 dc). Ch 4 (= 1st dc + 1 ch), (1 dc in next ch loop, ch 1, 1 dc in next dc, ch 1, 1 dc in next ch loop, ch 1, 1 dc in each of next 2 dc), ch 1; rep instructions within parentheses 2 more times. Ch 1, 1 dc in next ch loop, ch 1, 1 dc in next dc, ch 1, 1 dc n next ch loop, ch 1, 1 dc in next dc, ch 1, 1 sl st in the 3rd ch at beg of rnd = 20 dc total, some with and some without ch 1 in between.

Row 2: Ch 3 (= 1st dc), 1 dc in sl st, (ch 1, 2 dc in each of the next 3 dc, ch 1, 1 dc in each of the nest 2 dc); rep instructions within parentheses 2 more times. Ch 1, 2 dc in each of the next 3 dc, ch 1. End with 1 sl st into top of ch 3 at beg of rnd = 16 dc groups.

Row 3: 1 sl st into 1st ch loop, ch 3 + 2 dc + ch 3 + 3 dc in same loop, 1 sc in next ch loop (between 2–dc groups), *3 dc + ch 3 + 3 dc in next ch loop (= between 2-dc groups), 1 sc in next loop. Rep from * = 8 dc groups.

Crochet the other wing the same way.

Weave in all ends neatly on WS. Make a chain stitch hanging loop and sew it securely through the inside of the head. Sew on a halo if desired.

Large Christmas Bell

THIS FAST AND EASY-TO-CROCHET BELL WILL BE DECORATIVE WHETHER HANGING ON THE CHRISTMAS TREE OR IN A WINDOW. THE BELL HOLDS ITS SHAPE WELL BUT YOU CAN ALSO STARCH IT WITH A SUGAR SOLUTION.

Yarn: Fiol from Solberg Spinderi (CYCA #2 [sport/baby], 100% mercerized cotton, 185 yd/169 m / 50 g), small amount of White
Crochet Hook: U.S. size C-2 / 2.5 mm
Notions: A bead
Measurements: approx. 2¾ in / 7 cm high

Ch 6 and join into a ring with 1 sl st into 1st ch. Leave a long tail to make a hanging loop later.

Rnd 1: Ch 3 (= 1st dc), work 11 dc around ring = 12 dc; end with 1 sl st into top of ch 3 at beg of rnd.

Rnd 2: Ch 3 (= 1st dc), 1 dc in dc and then 2 dc in each dc around = 24 dc; end with 1 sl st into top of ch 3 at beg of rnd.

Rnds 3–7: Ch 3 (= 1st dc), 1 dc in next dc, (ch 1, 2 dc) around, ending with ch 1, 1 sl st into top of ch 3 at beg of rnd = 12 dc groups with ch 1 in between each.

Rnd 8: Ch 3 (= 1st dc), 2 dc in next dc, ch 1, (1 dc in next dc, 2 dc in next dc, ch 1) 12 times and end with 1 sl st into top of ch 3 at beg of rnd.

Rnd 9: (1 sc, 1 dc, 2 tr, 1 dc, 1 sc in same ch loop) 12 times; end with 1 sl st into top of ch 3 at beg of rnd.

Cut yarn and weave in ends on WS. If desired, attach a bead inside the bell.

To stiffen the bell, make a sugar solution (see page 164 in the Crochet School section). Soak bell well in solution.

Large Christmas bell

Smiley Face Purse

THIS SWEET CHILD'S PURSE IS CROCHETED SPIRALLY. IT GOES VERY QUICKLY SO WHY NOT MAKE SEVERAL IN A VARIETY OF COLORS?

Yarn: Muskat from Drops (CYCA #3 [DK/light worsted], 100% cotton, 109 yd/100m / 50 g), 50 g Pink
Crochet Hook: U. S. size C-2 / 2.5 mm
Notions: a zipper about 4 in / 10 cm long; small amount of black yarn for the mouth and eyes
Measurements: approx. 4 in / 10 cm in diameter

The bag is worked in a spiral (see page 154). Work all single crochet sts through both loops of stitch below (see page 144).

FRONT

Begin with a magic ring as described on page 147 and work 10 sc around ring. End with 1 sl st to 1st sc.

Rnd 1: Work 2 sc in each sc around = 20 sc.

Rnd 2: (1 sc in next sc, 2 sc in next sc) around = 30 sc.

Rnd 3: (1 sc in each of next 3 sc, 2 sc in next sc) around; end with 1 sc in each of last 2 sts = 37 sc.

Rnd 4: (1 sc in each of next 4 sc, 2 sc in next sc, 1 sc in each of next 3 sc, 2 sc in next sc) around; end with 1 sc in last st = 45 sc.

Rnd 5: 1 sc in each sc around.

Rnd 6: (1 sc in each of next 5 sc, 2 sc in next sc) around; end with 1 sc in each of last 3 sts = 52 sc.

Rnd 7: 1 sc in each sc around.

Rnd 8: (1 sc in each of next 6 sc, 2 sc in next sc) around; end with 1 sc in each of last 3 sts = 57 sc.

Rnd 9: 1 sc in each sc around.
Cut yarn.

BACK

Work as for front but do not cut yarn at end. Use the yarn to join the back to front and for a strap.

Finishing

Begin by crocheting the mouth: Hold the yarn at the WS of the front piece. Insert the hook between the 6th and 7th rnds and bring loop of yarn through. Insert the hook 1 sc further along and bring loop through stitch and through previous loop. Continue the same way until mouth is desired length.

EYES

Begin with a magic ring (see page 147) and work 10 sc around ring. Tighten sts to form a curved piece. Cut yarn and sew on eye by hand. Make and attach the other eye the same way.

Place the back and front together with WS facing WS. Join the pieces with sc through back loop, leaving an opening for the zipper. Sew in zipper by hand.

STRAP

Chain approx. 25 sts or enough for total length of strap. Attach last ch with 1 sc on the opposite side of the opening. Work 1 sc in each ch back.

Sweet Flower Purse

THIS BAG IS CROCHETED AS FOR THE SMILEY FACE PURSE ON PAGE 47. A COLORFUL FLOWER DECORATES THE FRONT.

Yarn: Pt Sumatra from Rauma (CYCA #4 [worsted/afghan/aran], 100% cotton, 93 yd/85 / 50 g), small amounts of Yellow, Light Pink, Red, Deep Rose, Green
Crochet Hook: U. S. size G-6 / 4 mm
Notions: a zipper about 4 in / 10 cm long
Measurements: approx. 4¼ in / 11 cm in diameter

Make the front and back as for the purse on page 47.

FLOWER
With Yellow, ch 7 and join into a ring with 1 sl st to 1st ch.

Rnd 1: Ch 3, work 17 dc around ring and join with 1 sl st to top of ch 3.

Rnd 2: Change to Light Pink. (1 sc, ch 3, skip 2 sts) 6 times = 6 ch loops. End with a sl st to first sc.

Rnd 3: 1 sl st into ch loop. In each of the ch-3 loops, work (1 sc, 5 dc, 2 sc).

Rnd 4: Change to Red. Work (1 sc behind petal in sc of Rnd 2, ch 5) 6 times = 6 ch loops. End with 1 sl st into ch loop.

Rnd 5: Work (1 sc, 7 dc, 1 sc) into each of the ch-6 loops.

Rnd 6: Change to Deep Rose. (1 sc behind and between petals, ch 7) 6 times. End with 1 sl st into 1st sc.

Rnd 7: Work (1 sc, 9 dc, 1 sc) into each of the ch-6 loops.

Rnd 8: Change to Green. (1 sc behind and between petals, ch 9) 6 times. End with 1 sl st into 1st sc.

Rnd 9: Work (1 sc, 11 dc, 1 sc) into each of the ch-6 loops. Cut yarn, leaving a long tail.

Using the end of the Yellow, sew on the rose at center front of bag. Weave in all but the Green ends on WS. Use tail of Green yarn to sew outer edge of rose to purse. Join and add zipper as for Smiley Face purse.

STRAP
Chain approx. 25 sts or enough for total length of strap. Attach last ch with 1 sc on the opposite side of the opening. Work 1 sc in each ch back.

Sweet flower purse

Cuddly Animals

CHILDREN WILL LOVE THESE ANIMALS BECAUSE THEY MAKE SOUNDS AND ARE NICE TO HOLD ONTO.

Pink Horse

Yarn: Mandarin Petit from SandnesGarn (CYCA #1 [sock/fingering/baby], 100% cotton, 195 yd/178 m / 50 g), 50 g Pink + small amounts White for the tail, mane, and foot soles
Crochet Hook: U.S. size C-2–D-3 / 2.5–3 mm
Notions: A round plastic box, half-filled with beads, fiber fill
Measurements: the horse is approx. 5¼ in / 13 cm long and 4 in / 10 cm tall

The horse is worked back and forth in single crochet.

With Pink, Ch 43.

Row 1: Insert hook into 4th ch from hook and sc; sc across = 40 sc.

Rows 2–7: Ch 2 (= 1st sc) and sc in each st across.

Row 8: 10 sl sts (up along one leg), and then sc 20 for back.

Rows 9–13: Sc 20 across each row; on the last row, end with ch 12 for front leg (see page 144 in the Crochet School section).

Row 14: Beginning in 3rd ch from hook, work 9 sc in ch, 10 sc across sc, ch 9 (for back neck), insert hook into next sc and then work 10 sc, ch 12 for other leg.

Rows 15–19: Beginning 3rd ch from hook, work sc over all the sts = 49 sc. *At the same time,* on each row, increase 1 sc in the center of the piece (over a chain st of the neck) for a total of 5 increases.

Row 20: Sl st up over front leg until 10 sts rem before the center of the piece, work 20 sc for the head; turn.

Row 21: Work 20 sc, ch 7 after the last sc for the horse's muzzle.

Row 22: 1 sc in each ch and then 20 sc, ch 7 after the last sc.

Row 23: Work 1 sc in each sc and then sc across, turning on last sc.

Rows 24–27: Begin rows with ch 2 and turn before last sc.

Row 28: Skip every other st to shape muzzle. Cut yarn.

HEAD

Row 1: Work 17 sc from the center of the piece and then ch 5 for the horse's chin.

Row 2: Beginning in 3rd ch from hook, work 19 sc, ch 5 for opposite side of chin.

Rows 3–5: Work as for Row 2, but turn 1 st from edge.

Row 6: Sc across, decreasing 3 sts evenly spaced across by skipping 1 st for each decrease. Cut yarn.

»——→

EARS (make 2 alike)
Ch 7, beginning in 3rd ch from hook, work 5 sc. Turn and work 3 dc in the center of the 5 sc, keep last loop on hook for each dc, yoh and bring through all loops at once.

Finishing
Sew on the ears and embroider an eye on each side of head with star stitch. Seam legs, underside of body, and hole in the back neck.

Mane: Cut two strands of White yarn, about 8 in / 20 cm long. Double strands and insert into a tapestry needle. Insert needle through the edge, beginning at lower part of back neck, and loop yarn ends through to tie mane to horse. Continue up back neck with several "knots" of mane.

Filling: Roll the box of beads in the fiber fill and fill the horse, with the box centered in the body. Seam the opening. Finish by seaming front neck and muzzle.

TAIL
Cut 9 strands about 6 in / 15 cm long. Using a tapestry needle, attach them to back of horse. Tie a firm knot at the base of the tail.

FOOT SOLES
Rnd 1: With White, work sc as tightly as possible around the opening on each leg.

Rnd 2: Work in sc around, skipping every other sc at the center. Weave in ends to WS.

Elephants

Yarn:
Small elephant:
Mandarin Petit from SandnesGarn (CYCA #1 [sock/fingering/baby], 100% cotton, 195 yd/178 m / 50 g), 50 g Purple + small amounts White for the eyes and foot soles

Large elephant:
Pt Petunia from Rauma (CYCA #3 [DK/light worsted], 100% cotton, 120 yd/110 m / 50 g), 50 g Turquoise and small amounts of dark Turquoise for the ears, tale and foot soles; a little bit of Blue for the eyes
Crochet Hook: *Small elephant:* U.S. size C-2 / 2.5 mm; *large elephant:* U.S. size E-4–G-6 / 3.5–4 mm
Notions: A round plastic box, half-filled with beads, fiber fill
Measurements: *Small elephant:* approx. 4 in / 10 cm long x 3½ in / 9 cm tall; *large elephant:* approx. 6 in / 15 cm long x 5½ in / 14 cm tall

Ch 42.

Row 1: Beginning in 3rd ch from hook, sc across = 41 sc.

Row 2: Ch 2, 19 sc, 2 sc in next sc, 20 sc.

Rows 3–6: Work as for Row 2, increasing the same way at center of back = 24 sc on each side.

Row 7: 10 sl sts (up along one back leg), and then continue with ch 2, 24 sc.

Rows 8–10: Ch 2, 24 sc.

Row 11: Ch 12 after the last sc for one front leg.

Row 12: Beginning in 3rd ch from hook, work 1 sc in each ch and then sc across back. Ch 12 after last sc.

Row 13: Beginning in 3rd ch from hook, work 1 sc in each ch. Continue with 1 sc in each sc across.

Rows 14–18: Ch 2 and sc across each row.

Row 19 (head): Sl st 10 along front leg until 10 sc rem.

Row 20–21: Ch 2; beginning in 2nd st, work 20 sc (= 21 sc total) to the center of the head, skip next sc, continue with sc across (**NOTE:** Decrease the same way—by skipping 1 sc at the center of the head—on all of the following rows).

Row 22: Work as for Row 21, but end with ch 12 for trunk.

Row 23: Insert hook into 3rd ch from hook and work 10 sc back, ending with ch 12 for trunk.

Rows 24–25: Beginning in 3rd ch from hook, sc across.

Rows 26–27: Ch 2; beginning in 2nd st, sc across to trunk on the opposite side.

Row 28: Ch 2; beginning in 2nd st, work 15 sc (= 16 sc over forehead). Cut yarn and bring end through last loop.

EARS
Ch 12

Row 1: Beginning in 3rd ch from hook, work 9 sc across.

Rows 2–4: Work 10 sc across each row.

Row 5: Increase 3 sc evenly spaced across row. Cut yarn and bring end through last loop.

TAIL
Chain 3 lengths for the tail. Using a tapestry needle, attach them to back of elephant. Braid the strands and tie a firm knot at the end of the tail, leaving a little tassel at tail end.

FINISHING
Sew on the ears and embroider an eye on each side of head with star stitch. Seam the legs and underside of body.

Filling: Roll the box of beads in the fiber fill and fill the elephant, with the box centered in the body. Seam the opening. Finish by seaming neck and trunk.

FOOT SOLES
Rnd 1: With White, work sc as tightly as possible around the opening on each leg.

Rnd 2: Work in sc around, skipping every other sc at the center. Weave in ends to WS.
Cut yarn and use end to tighten the hole at center of sole.

Shell-Stitch Coverlet

THIS IS A QUICK-TO-CROCHET PATTERN THAT IS ALSO SUITABLE FOR A SHAWL, SCARF, OR BABY CARRIAGE COVERLET. IT IS EASY TO ADJUST THE WIDTH FOR WHATEVER PROJECT YOU CHOOSE.

Yarn: Fine Alpaca (Tynn Alpakka) from Du Store Alpakka (CYCA #1 [sock/fingering/baby], 100% alpaca, 183 yd/167 m / 50 g)

Yarn Amounts: 100 g of **Color 1**, Light Pink and 50 g of **Color 2**, Deep Rose

Crochet Hook: U.S. size G-6 / 4 mm

Measurements: approx. 13¾ x 19¾ in / 35 x 50 cm

Pattern: If you want to adjust the pattern, begin with a chain that is a multiple of 14 + 1 sts.

Elongated Double Crochet: When bringing yarn around hook and forming stitch, pull so loop is ⅝ in / 1.5 cm long.

With Color 1, ch 85.

Row 1: Work 1 sc in 2nd ch from hook, *skip 6 ch, work 13 elongated dc in next st, skip 6 ch, 1 sc in next st; from * across.

Row 2: Ch 4, 1 elongated dc in sc, *ch 5 , 1 sc in the 7th of the elongated dc group, ch 5, 2 elongated in 1 sc; rep from * across, ending with ch 1.

Row 3: *1 sc between the 2 elongated dc, 13 elongated dc in sc between the dc of previous row; rep from * and end with 1 sc between the elongated dc and ch.

Repeat Rows 2 and 3 until piece is desired length.

EDGING (worked all around)

Rnd 1 (Color 1): Work 1 rnd in sc with 3 sc in each corner; end with 1 sl st into 1st sc.

Rnd 2 (Color 2): Begin with ch 1 at first st of previous rnd (= 1st sc), skip 3 sc, *13 elongated dc in next sc, skip 3 sc; rep from * around and end with 1 sl st into 1st ch.

Weave in all ends neatly on WS.

Shell-stitched coverlet

Retro Tunic

THIS TUNIC IS A MIX OF OLD AND NEW STYLES THAT MEET IN PERFECT HARMONY. THE TUNIC IS CROCHETED FROM THE TOP DOWN, WITH THE YOKE WORKED BACK AND FORTH AND THE REST IN THE ROUND.

Sizes: 6-9 months (1-2, 3-4 years)

Finished Measurements:

Total length: 14¼ (16½, 18¼) in / 36 (42, 46) cm or desired length

Chest (as measured below yoke): 21¾ (23¼, 25¼) in / 55 (59, 64) cm

Yarn: Merino Extra Fine from Drops (CYCA #3 [DK/light worsted], 100% Merino wool, 115 yd/105 m / 50 g)

Yarn Amounts:

50 g each of **Color 1:** Light Gray-Green or Light Pink and **Color 2:** Mustard or Light Yellow 150 (200, 250) g **Color 3:** Brown or Light Brown

Notions: 3 buttons

Crochet Hook: U.S. size 7 / 4.5 mm

Gauge: 18 dc = 4 in / 10 cm. Adjust hook size to obtain correct gauge if necessary.

NOTES: The colors change on every row of the yoke in the following sequence: Color 1, Color 2, Color 3, Color 1, Color 2, Color 3, etc. Cut yarn each time you change colors and catch the "old" color as you work (see page 152 in the Crochet School section).

There will be a little jog at the center back as you crochet around in double crochet and end each round. To avoid the jog, you can work the entire tunic back and forth and seam it up center back when finishing.

Crab Stitch (also called reverse single crochet): Crab stitch is single crochet worked from left to right as follows: Do not turn work at the end of a right side row. Instead, hold work with RS facing you and hold crochet hook at the left side. *Insert the hook through both loops of the first st to the right, turn the hook downwards to pick up the yarn for a yarnover and bring it through the loops. Yoh and bring yarn through both loops on the hook. Repeat from *.

Double Crochet Fan (dc fan): (3 dc, ch 3, 3 dc) into one st or chain loop.

With Color 1, ch 70.

Row 1: Beginning in 2nd ch from hook, work 69 sc.

Row 2 (RS): Change to Color 2 and ch 3 (= 1st dc), 1 dc in each of the 3 first sts, *skip 3 sts, work dc fan in next st, skip 3 sts, work 1 dc in each of the next 4 sts; rep from * across (= 6 dc fans).

»⟶

Row 3: Change to Color 3 and work in crab st from left to right. Begin with ch 1 and then work 1 crab st into each dc and 3 crab sts in each ch loop.

Row 4: Change to Color 1. Begin with ch 3 (= 1st dc), work 1 dc in each of the first 2 sts of previous row by inserting hook into back loop of crab st. This method allows the crab sts to be a little raised on the RS of the work. Work 2 dc in 3rd st. *Skip 3 sts, work dc fan around loop of crab st; skip 3 sts, work 2 dc in first st and then 1 dc in each of next 2 sts, 2 dc in last st (= 6 dc). Repeat from *. End row by skipping 3 sts, work dc fan in loop of crab st, skip 3 sts, 2 dc in 1st st, dc to end of row. This sequence adds 1 dc on each side of center back, while, on the rest of the row, there will be 2 new sts in each dc section.

Repeat Rows 3 and 4.

Repeat the yoke sequence until there are 14 (16, 18 dc in each dc section of the yoke (9 dc each at beginning and end of row). End with Row 3, Color 1.

Body of Tunic (worked in the round)

Continue with Color 3 only; begin rounds at center back: Ch 3 (=1st dc), 22 (25, 28) dc, (work 3 dc in each of the ch loops), ch 5 (5, 5), skip 27

(29, 31) crab sts, work 42 (46, 50) dc, ch 5 (5, 5), skip 27 (29, 31) crab sts, work 23 (26, 29) dc. End rnd with 1 sl st into top of ch 3 at beg of rnd.

On every 4th rnd, increase 3 times by working the 3 center sts at each side as follows: 2 dc in 1st st, 1 dc in 2nd st, 2 dc in 3rd st. Continue working as set until tunic is 2 in / 5 cm shorter than total length as measured from underarm.

LOWER EDGE
Change to Color 1 and work in crab st around (from left to right). Change to Color 3 and work in dc (from right to left) around. Change to Color 2 and work crab st around. Change to Color 1 and work in dc around. Change to Color 3 and work in crab st around. Change to Color 2 and work in dc around. Change to Color 1 and work in crab st around.

Cut yarn and weave in all ends on WS.

Edging around center back placket: With Color 1, work in sc around center back opening, making 3 button loops evenly spaced on one side = ch 3 for each loop. Sew on buttons.

Carriage Blanket

THIS BLANKET CONSISTS OF 5 X 7 SQUARES AND IS FINISHED WITH A WIDE DOUBLE CROCHET EDGING ALL AROUND.

Yarn: Lerke from Dale Garn, (CYCA #3 [DK/light worsted], 52% Merino wool/48% cotton, 125 yd/114 m / 50 g), approx. 100 g each of 5 colors. Arrange your own bouquet of colors.
Crochet Hook: U.S. size E-4 / 3.5 mm
Measurements: 23¾ x 31½ in / 60 x 80 cm

Ch 8 and join into a ring with 1 sl st to 1st ch.

Rnd 1: Ch 6, (1 dc in ring, ch 3) 7 times and end with 1 sl st into 3rd ch at beginning of rnd (= 8 ch loops). Cut yarn and change colors.

Rnd 2: Attach new color with 1 sl st around 1st ch loop, ch 3, 3 dc around same loop, (ch 2, 4 dc in next loop) 7 times and end with ch 2, 1 sl st into top of ch 3 at beginning of rnd. Cut yarn and change colors.

Rnd 3: Attach new color with 1 sl st around 1st ch, ch 3, 5 dc in same loop, (ch 1, 6 dc around next loop, ch 3, 6 dc around next loop) 3 times. End with ch 1, 6 dc around next loop, ch 3. End with 1 sl st into top of ch 3 at beginning of rnd. Cut yarn and change colors.

Rnd 4: Attach new color with 1 sl st around 1st ch, *ch 3, 1 sc between the 3rd and 4th dc in group, ch 3, (2 dc, ch 3, 2 dc) in ch-3 loop (= corner), ch 3, 1 sc between the 3rd and 4th dc in group, ch 3, 1 sc in ch loop; rep from * 3 more times, but omit last sc and end with 1 sl st into 1st ch. Cut yarn and change colors.

Rnd 5: Attach new color with 1 sl st around 1st ch, *ch 3, 2 dc in ch loop of previous rnd. Continue, working 3 dc in each ch loop around with 5 dc in each corner. End with 1 sl st into 3rd ch at beginning of rnd. Cut yarn and fasten off ends.

Finishing
With RS facing, join two squares with sc so there will be a raised edge between the squares. Join squares until you have a strip with 5 squares and then make 6 more strips the same way. Join the strips as you joined the squares.

Edge the blanket with 1 rnd dc in each of the colors. Each rnd begins with ch 3 (= 1st dc) and ends with 1 sl st into top of ch 3 at beginning of rnd. Work 3 dc in each corner. The first rnd should have about 90 dc across the width and 130 dc along the length. Change colors on each round until you've worked 1 rnd with each color.

Cut yarn and weave in ends on WS.

Striped Baby Cardigans

SIMPLE, SWEET, STRIPED BABY CARDIGANS FOR BOYS AND GIRLS. THESE CARDIGANS CAN EASILY BE SIZED UP IF YOU WANT. THEY ARE WORKED BACK AND FORTH FROM THE SLEEVE CUFF TO CENTER BACK.

Size: 3 months
Finished Measurements:
Chest: approx. 21¾ in / 55 cm
Total length: approx. 9¾ in / 25 cm
Sleeve length: approx. 6 in / 15 cm

Yarn: Mandarin Petit from SandnesGarn (CYCA #1 [sock/fingering/baby], 100% cotton, 195 yd/178 m / 50 g)
Yarn Amounts: 50 g each of:

Colorway A	Colorway B
Color 1: Deep Rose	**Color 1:** Blue
Color 2: Yellow	**Color 2:** Green
Color 3: Green	**Color 3:** Turquoise
Color 4: Orange	

Notions: 6 buttons
Crochet Hook: U.S. size D-3 / 3 mm
Gauge: 20 dc = 4 in / 10 cm across width. Adjust hook size to obtain correct gauge if necessary.

Stripes

With each color, work 2 rows of dc, either with Colorway A, Colors 1–4, or Colorway B, Colors 1–3.
At the end of each sleeve, work only 1 row dc with Color 1.

LEFT HALF OF CARDIGAN

With Color 1, ch 34 for sleeve. Beginning in 4th ch from hook, dc across = 32 dc. Work back and forth in stripe pattern over these 32 sts until there are 17 rows of dc (or to desired sleeve length). *At the same time,* increase 1 st at each side on every 5th row. Cut yarn.

Loosely ch 32 (= side seam) and continue over the sleeve sts (= 38 sts), ch 34 (side seam at front); turn.
Beginning in 4th ch from hook, work in dc across = 102 dc. Work 9 more rows (= 10 rows total).

Now shape neck: Turn and work back over sts of back (= 44 dc). Turn and work back. Work a total of 5 rows in dc over the 44 sts. Cut yarn. Now work on the front: skip 16 dc at shoulder. Begin with ch 3 in 17th dc and work downwards on front (a total of 42 dc). Work 4 more rows over these sts = half of cardigan. On the last row, make buttonholes for a girl's cardigan (see details in next paragraph).

Work the right side of the cardigan as for left, but, on the last row, make 6 buttonholes for a boy's cardigan, evenly spaced as follows: 2 dc, skip 1 dc, ch 1, (8 dc, skip 1 dc, ch 1) 6 times (for 6 buttonholes) and end with 3 dc. Cut yarn and fasten off.

Finishing

Seam the two halves of the back. Seam sides and sleeves (see page 161, "Edges and Joining," in the Crochet School section).

Edge the cardigan with Edging 5 (see page 141.

Striped baby cardigans

Child's Dress with Crochet Yoke

THIS MUST-HAVE DRESS IS SO PRETTY WITH ITS CROCHETED YOKE AND LACE EDGING ON A FABRIC SKIRT. THE FABRIC/CROCHET COMBINATION IS PERFECT. [Design: Kari Haugen for Dale Garn AS]

Size: 6 (12, 24, 36) months

Finished Measurements:

Chest: approx. 17¼ (19¼, 21¼, 22) in / 44 (49, 54, 56) cm

Total length: approx. 13½ (15½, 18½, 19¾) in / 34 (39, 47, 50) cm

Yarn: Vipe from Dale Garn (CYCA #2 [sport/baby], 100% cotton, 137 yd/125 m / 50 g),

Yarn Amounts: 100 (100, 150, 150) g Raspberry or Mint

Notions: 3-4 buttons; fabric, for example fine cotton. Fabric amounts include seam allowances for one side, the top and folded lower edge: Width approx. 35½ (39½, 43¼, 47¼) in / 90 (100, 110, 120) cm and length approx. 8¾ (9½, 11¾, 12¼) in / 22 (24, 30, 31) cm.

Crochet Hook: U.S. size C-2 / 2.5 mm

Gauge: 29 sts = 4 in / 10 cm

Yoke: 1 repeat (= 1 dc group) in pattern = approx. 1 in / 2.5 cm

Edging: 24 sc = 4 in / 10 cm

Adjust hook size to obtain correct gauge if necessary.

Pattern:

Row 1: Beginning in 3rd ch from hook, work in sc across.

Row 2: Turn with ch 1, *skip 2 sts, work 5 dc in same st, skip 2 sts, 1 sc; rep from * across.

Row 3: Turn with ch 3, *(3 dc, ch 1, 3 dc) in 3rd st of 5-dc group; rep from * across and end with 1 sc in 5th st of dc group.

Row 4: Turn with ch 3, *(3 dc, ch 1, 3 dc) in ch loop of dc group below; rep from * across and end with 1 sc in 6th st of last group.

Repeat Rows 1–4.

NOTES:

At beginning of row, work half a dc group as follows: Ch 4, 3 dc in ch loop.

At end of row, work half a dc group as follows: 3 dc, ch 1, 1 dc.

Work whole dc groups within the row: Begin with 1 sc between groups.

FRONT

Ch 55 (61, 67, 73) and work in pattern as described above. Work back and forth with 9 (10, 11, 12) dc groups [= 5 (6, 7, 8) rows].

Shape armholes: Cut yarn and re-attach at right side, with RS facing. Begin in the 2nd (2nd, 2nd, 3rd) dc group and work a half (half, half, whole) dc group. Continue in pattern to the opposite side and end as for beginning of row. Work a total of 4 (4, 5, 5) rows the same way.

»⟶

⇻ 65 ⇺

Child's dress with crochet yoke

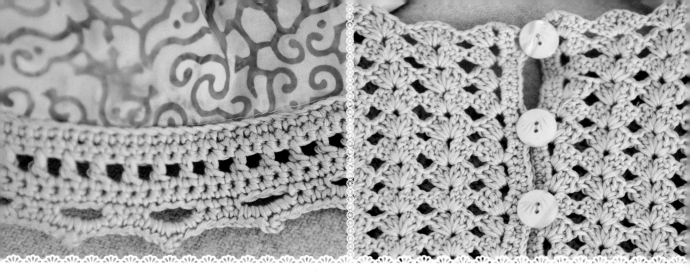

Shape shoulder: Begin on right side. Work a half + whole (half + whole, half + whole + half, whole + whole) dc group for 4 (5, 5, 6) rows. Work left shoulder the same way, reversing shaping.

RIGHT BACK

Ch 28 (31, 34, 37); turn and work in pattern as for the front.
NOTE: At center back, work half dc groups for sizes 6 and 24 months.

Shape right armhole as for front. Work another 6 (6, 7, 8) rows for back neck. Work shoulder as for front = 2 (2, 3, 3) rows.

LEFT BACK

Work as for right back, reversing shaping.

LOWER EDGING FOR SKIRT

Ch 212 (236, 260, 284).

Row 1: 1 sc in 2nd ch from hook. Work a total of 211 (234, 259, 283) sc across. Make sure that the edging will fit all around the skirt—the edging should not pull in.

Row 2: Turn with ch 1 and work the same number of sc as for Row 1.

Row 3: Turn with ch 4, skip 2 sts, 1 dc in next st; (ch 1, skip 1 st, 1 dc) across.

Row 4: Turn with ch 1, 1 sc in 1st dc; (1 sc in next ch loop, 1 sc in next st) across, ending with

1 sc in last ch loop + 1 sc in 3rd ch of the 4 ch at beginning of Row 3.

Row 5: Turn with ch 1 and sc across.

Row 6: Turn with ch 1, 3 sc; (ch 4, skip 3 sts, 1 sc in each of next 3 sts) across, ending with ch 4, skip 3 sts, 1 sc in last st.

Row 7: Turn with ch 1, *(3 sc, ch 3, 3 sc) in ch loop, 1 sc in each of next 3 sts; rep from * across.

Finishing
Place the crocheted yoke pieces with RS facing RS and sew or crochet them together with slip sts along the shoulders and sides. Begin on the WS, crochet a sc edging back and forth on the right side of back. On the left side, work 1 row sc on WS, turn and sc back. *At the same time*, evenly spaced, make 3-4 button loops of ch 5 each. Lightly steam press yoke.

SKIRT

Fold the fabric in half with the WS facing out and seam by machine at center back. Overcast the seam and top edge. Gather the fabric in to fit the yoke. Place the fabric under the yoke with RS facing out and with the seam at center back. Pin and then machine-stitch on RS.

Double fold the hem of the skirt with each fold about ⅜ in / 1 cm deep. Pin the crocheted edging to RS of fabric and then sew on.

*Child's dress
with crochet yoke*

Viking Sweater

A SIMPLE SWEATER TO CROCHET AND VERY EASY TO ADJUST FOR MORE
SIZES THAN GIVEN HERE. THE SWEATER MIGHT REMIND YOU A LITTLE
OF A COAT OF ARMOR FROM THE VIKING PERIOD. IT HAS COMPLETELY
STRAIGHT LINES, WITH A NECK PLACKET AND A SLIT AT EACH SIDE.

Sizes: 1-2 (3-4) years
Finished Measurements:
Chest: 23¾ (26¾) in / 60 (68) cm
Total length: 13½ (15¾) in / 34 (40) cm
Sleeve length: 9 (10¾) in / 23 (27) cm

Yarn: Fine Alpaca (Tynn Alpakka) from Du Store Alpakka (CYCA #1 [sock/fingering/baby], 100% alpaca, 183 yd/167 m / 50 g)
Yarn Amounts:
100 g **of Color 1:** Gray-Brown OR Dark Green
150 g **of Color 2:** Sand OR Gray-Green
100 g **of Color 3:** Light Gray OR Light Gray-Green
Crochet Hook: U.S. size G-6 and 7 / 4 and 4.5 mm
Gauge: 15 dc in width and 9 rows in length with larger size hook = 4 x 4 in / 10 x 10 cm. Adjust hook sizes to obtain correct gauge if necessary.

The sweater is constructed in four pieces: 1 front, 1 back, and 2 sleeves

BACK
With larger size hook and 2 strands of Color 1 held together, ch 47 (57). Beginning in 4th ch from hook, work 45 (55) dc across. Work 6 (7) rows each (dc across all rows) in the following color sequence:
A—2 strands of Color 1
B—1 strand each of Color 1 and Color 2
C—2 strands of Color 2
D—1 strand each of Color 2 and Color 3
E—2 strands of Color 3
Cut yarn.

FRONT
Work as for back, but after 20 (24) rows, divide the front at the center for the placket. Work each side separately until 3 (4) rows remain in color striping.

Neck shaping: Work only over the 12 (15)

outermost dc at each side until finished length. Cut yarn.

SLEEVES
With larger size hook and 2 strands of Color 1 held together, ch 32 (37). Beginning in 4th ch from hook, work 30 (35) dc across. Work 4 (5) rows each (dc across all rows) in the color sequence, but, for size 3-4 years, work only 4 rows of the last 2 color stripes.
At the same time, increase 1 st at each side on every row with a change of color (= 4 sts increased at each side of each sleeve). There should be 38 (43) dc across top of each sleeve. Cut yarn.

Finishing
Weave in all ends on WS. With RS facing, 2 strands of Color 3 held together, and smaller size hook, crochet the front and back pieces together at the shoulders with sc. Lay the body flat and pin in one sleeve, with center of sleeve top at shoulder seam. Crochet sleeve to body and then attach the other sleeve the same way. Fold the sweater with the front against the back. Beginning at lower edge on inside of one sleeve, crochet the pieces together upwards. Continue down the long sides, stopping before the bottom color stripe for the slit. Work sc down the slit on the front, around and up slit at opposite side and then seam the other side above the slit. Sc down along slit at back and then around and up slit on opposite side.

NECK EDGING
Beginning at center of back neck, work in sc to the beginning of the front placket. Ch 30 for a tie. Turn and insert hook into 2nd ch from hook and then sc back along chain. Continue in sc down placket and then up other side. Make a cord as for the first one. Finish with sc around to center back neck.

Cut yarn and weave in all ends on WS.

»—→

Fox Scarf

THE FOX MOTIF IS A SURE WINNER. THE SCARF IS SOFT AND SO FUN!

Yarn: Soft Alpaca from SandnesGarn (CYCA #5 [chunky/craft/rug], 80% baby alpaca/20% acrylic, 109 yd/100 m / 50 g)
Yarn Amounts: 100 g Rust Red and a small amount of White + Black for the snout and eyes
Crochet Hook: U.S. sizes H-8 and E-4 / 5 and 3.5 mm
Gauge: 10 dc = 4 in / 10 cm.
Adjust hook sizes to obtain correct gauge if necessary.
Measurements: Length: approx. 25½ in / 65 cm; width: approx. 4 in / 10 cm

SCARF

With larger hook and Rust Red, ch 20 and join into a ring with 1 sl st into 1st ch.

Rnd 1: Ch 3 (= 1st dc), dc around, ending with 1 sl st into top of ch 3 = 20 dc.
Repeat Rnd 1 until scarf is approx. 25½ in / 65 cm long or desired length.

PAWS

With smaller hook and Rust Red, ch 12.

Row 1: Beginning in 3rd ch from hook, work 1 sc in each ch across = 10 sc.

Rows 2–10: Work back and forth in sc.
Now begin working in rounds (count rounds, not rows).

Rnd 11: Change to White and work around in sc; join into a ring with 1 sl st into 1st sc.

Rnds 12–13: Ch 2, 9 sc, and end with 1 sl st into top of ch 2.

Rnds 14–15: Decrease by skipping every other st around. Cut yarn and make 3 more paws the same way.

TAIL

Work as for a paw but begin with ch 10 and increase 2 sts on the next row by working 2 sc each into the 2nd and next-to-last sts.

Change to White after 12 rows and continue working back and forth. Skip 1 sc at each side until no more sts rem.

HEAD

Make a magic ring as described on page 147. With Rust Red and smaller hook, work 10 sc around ring; join with 1 sl st into 1st sc.

Rnd 1: Work 2 sc in each sc around = 20 sc.

Rnd 2: Work (1 sc in next st, 2 sc in next st) around = 30 sc.

Rnd 3: Work (1 sc in each of next 3 sts, 2 sc in next st) around; end with 1 sc in each of last 2 sts = 37 sts.

Rnd 4: Work (1 sc in each of next 4 sts, 2 sc in next st, work 2 sc in each of next 3 dc, 2 sc in next st) around; end with 1 sc in last st = 45 sc.

Rnd 5: Sc in each st around.

Rnd 6: Work (1 sc in each of next 5 sts, 2 sc in next st) around and end with 1 sc in each of last 3 sts = 52 sts.

Rnd 7: Sc in each st around.

Rnd 8: Work (1 sc in each of next 9 sts, 2 sc in next st) around and end with 1 sc in each of last 2 sts = 57 sts.
If the head does not yet have a diameter of 4 in / 10 cm, continue around in sc.

WHITE FACE

With smaller size hook and White, ch 8.

Row 1: Beginning in 4th ch from hook, work 4 sc and end with ch 5.

Row 2: Beginning in 4th ch from hook, sc across, ending with ch 5.

Rows 3–4: Work as for Row 2.

Rows 5–6: Work 1 sc in each sc across.

Row 7: Divide the piece at the center and work 2 rows sc on each half.

»———→

SNOUT

With smaller size hook and Black, ch 4; join into a ring with 1 sl st into 1st ch.

Rnd 1: Work 10 sc around ring and end with 1 sl st into 1st sc. Cut yarn.

EYES

Work as for snout but do not cut yarn. Ch 3, 2 dc in each sc of previous rnd. Keeping loops on the hook, cut yarn and pull through all loops at once with 1 sl st. Make another eye the same way.

EARS

With larger hook and Rust Red, ch 13.

Row 1: Beginning in 4th ch from hook, work 9 sc.

Rows 2–5: Ch 3 (= 1st dc); work across in dc, skipping the last st on each row.

At the end, make a tight row of sc around the ear, with 2 sc at the tip. Cut yarn and make another ear the same way.

Finishing

Seam each paw at the side. Attach 2 paws to one end of the scarf. Seam the tail and attach it to the opposite end. Sew on the head a little skewed at one ear and the center of the face so that it will be positioned correctly when you pull it through scarf ends.

Sew on the other 2 paws a little behind the body.

Bear Scarf

ADORABLE AND WARM, FOR CHILDREN!

Sizes: 3 (8) years
Measurements: Length: approx. 17 ¾ (25½) in / 45 (65) cm; width: approx. 4 in / 10 cm (both sizes)

Yarn: Soft Alpaca from SandnesGarn (CYCA #5 [chunky/craft/rug], 80% baby alpaca/20% acrylic, 109 yd/100 m / 50 g)
Yarn Amounts: 100 g White + Black for the snout, mouth, and eyes
Crochet Hook: U.S. sizes H-8 and E-4 / 5 and 3.5 mm
Gauge: 10 dc = 4 in / 10 cm.
Adjust hook sizes to obtain correct gauge if necessary.

The scarf is worked with the larger hook and all the details with the smaller hook.

SCARF

With larger hook and White, ch 20 and join into a ring with 1 sl st into 1st ch.

Rnd 1: Ch 3 (= 1st dc), work 1 dc in each ch around and end with 1 sl st into top of ch 3 = 20 dc.

Rnd 2: Ch 3 (= 1st dc), work dc around = 20 dc. Repeat Rnd 2 until scarf is finished length.

End by cutting yarn, leaving a long enough length for sewing up; bring yarn through last loop.

HEAD

With White and smaller hook, ch 4; join with 1 sl st into 1st ch.

Rnd 1: Ch 1 (=1st sc), 7 sc around ring; end with 1 sl st into 1st ch = 8 sc.

Bear scarf

Rnd 2: Ch 1 (=1st sc), 1 sc in same st, 2 sc in each st around; end with 1 sl st into 1st ch = 16 sc.

Rnd 3: Ch 1 (=1st sc), 1 sc in each sc around; end with 1 sl st into 1st ch = 16 sc.

Rnd 4: Ch 1 (=1st sc), 1 sc in same st, and then 2 sc in each st around; end with 1 sl st into 1st ch = 32 sc.

Rnd 5: Ch 1 (=1st sc), 1 sc in each sc around; end with 1 sl st into 1st ch = 32 sc.

Rnd 6: Ch 1 (=1st sc), 1 sc in each of next 6 sc, 2 sc in next st, (1 sc in each of next 7 sc, 2 sc in next st) 3 times = 36 sc.

Rnds 7–8: Work as for Rnd 6, with 1 more st between each increase.

Cut yarn, leaving a tail long enough for sewing up later.

EARS
With White and smaller hook, ch 3; join with 1 sl st into 1st ch.

Rnd 1: Ch 3 (= 1st dc), work 11 dc around ring = 12 dc total. Bring yarn through last st without tightening loop. Cut yarn. Make another ear the same way.

SNOUT
With White and smaller hook, ch 3; join with 1 sl st into 1st ch.

Rnd 1: Ch 1 (=1st sc), 8 sc around ring; end with 1 sl st into 1st ch = 9 sc.

Rnd 2: Ch 1 (=1st sc), 1 sc in same st, and then 2 sc in each st around; end with 1 sl st into 1st ch = 18 sc.

Rnd 3: Ch 1 (=1st sc), (1 sc in each of next 2 sts, 2 sc in next st) around; end with 1 sl st into 1st ch = 24 sc.

Rnd 3: Ch 1 (=1st sc), 1 sc in each sc around; end with 1 sl st into 1st ch = 24 sc.

LEGS (make 4 alike)
With White and smaller hook, ch 3; join with 1 sl st into 1st ch.

Rnd 1: Ch 1 (=1st sc), 4 sc around ring; end with 1 sl st into 1st ch = 5 sc.

Rnd 2: Ch 1 (=1st sc), 1 sc in same st, 2 sc in each st around; end with 1 sl st into 1st ch = 10 sc.

Rnds 3–12: Ch 1 (=1st sc), 1 sc in each sc around; end with 1 sl st into 1st ch. Cut yarn.

ROUND TAIL
With White and smaller hook, ch 3; join with 1 sl st into 1st ch.

Rnd 1: Ch 1 (=1st sc), 8 sc around ring; end with 1 sl st into 1st ch = 9 sc.
Work around and around in sc until you have formed a little ball.

Finishing
Begin by making a snout with black yarn as for the tail but work only 1 rnd.

Embroider the mouth and eyes with black yarn on the muzzle.

Sew the muzzle to the head and then sew on the ears firmly at an angle to the head.

Sew on two legs to each end of the scarf. Sew the tail onto the back about 2½–4 in / 6–10 cm from lower edge.

Bear scarf

Cool Vest

A SHARP-LOOKING VEST THAT CAN EASILY BECOME A SWEET AND
PRETTY GARMENT IN SOFTER COLORS. THE VEST IS CROCHETED
WITH TWO STRANDS OF YARN HELD TOGETHER.

Sizes: 6-9 months (1, 2, 4 years)

Finished Measurements:

Chest: 20½ (22¾, 24½, 26¾) in / 52 (58, 62, 68) cm

Length: approx. 11 (12¾, 14¼, 15¾) in / 28 (32, 36, 40) cm as measured from the center of shoulder, when completed and buttoned

Yarn: Fabel from Drops (CYCA #1 [sock/fingering/baby], 75% wool/25% nylon, 224 yd/205 m/50 g)

Yarn Amounts:

100 g **Color 1:** Blue

50 g each of

Color 2: Blue/Gray

Color 3: Royal Blue

Color 4: Light Gray [Alpaca Mix from Drops (CYCA #2 [sport/baby], 100% alpaca, 182 yd/166 m / 50 g)]

Notions: 4 buttons, approx. ⅜ in / 1 cm in diameter

Crochet Hook: U.S. size 7 / 4.5 mm

Gauge: 15 dc = 4 in / 10 cm.

Adjust hook size to obtain correct gauge if necessary.

Tip

To avoid having to weave in all the ends from the color changes later on, work as follows: Ch 3 (= 1st dc) with the new color. Lay the old color beside the new color along the top of previous row. Work 5–7 dc over both strands. Continue with new color only.

NOTE: Always hold 2 strands of yarn together.

BACK

With Color 1, ch 42 (46, 50, 54).

Row 1: Beginning in 4th ch from hook, work 39 (43, 47, 51) dc across = 40 (44, 48, 52) dc total.

Row 2: Change to Color 2. Begin with ch 3 (= 1st dc) and then work dc across.

Row 3: Change to Color 3 and work as for Row 2.

Row 4: Change to Color 4 and work as for Row 2.

Continue as set, changing colors in the sequence 1, 2, 3, 4 on every row, until piece measures 8 (8¾, 9½, 10¼) in / 20 (22, 24, 26) cm. With Color 1, work 1 row dc.

Shape armholes: Sl st over the first 3 dc (all sizes) and then ch 3 (= 1st dc), work in dc until 3 sts rem; turn. 1 sl st into 1st dc and then work in dc across until 1 st rem; turn. Repeat the second decrease row 2 more times for sizes 6-9 months (1, 2 years) = 6 sts total decreased at each side. Size 4 years: repeat the second decrease row 3 more times = 7 sts total decreased at each side.

Now work 4 (4, 5, 5) rows over rem sts. Finish with 4 rows dc over the outermost 8 (8, 10, 10) sts at each side for shoulder straps.

FRONT

Work as for back until 1 row past armhole shaping. Beginning at one side, work 10 (10, 12, 12) dc; turn and work 1 sl st into 1st dc and complete row. Turn and work 9 (9, 11, 11) dc; turn and work 1 sl st into 1st dc and complete row = 8 (8, 10, 10) dc rem. Continue rows in dc until 2 rows shorter than back (or to length desired). Work opposite side the same way.

Finishing

Seam sides. Weave in all ends not previously crocheted in. Sew 2 buttons to each shoulder strap on the back. The front flaps are buttoned in the last dc row so you don't need a flap over the shoulders. Make sure the buttons are small enough to go through the openings between double crochet sts.

Baby Cardigan

THIS CARDIGAN IS WORKED IN ONE PIECE AND IS A GREAT PROJECT FOR BEGINNERS. THERE IS NO RIGHT OR WRONG SIDE—IT'S JUST THE SAME ON BOTH SIDES. TO FINISH, YOU CAN CHOOSE WHETHER TO PLACE THE BUTTONHOLES ON THE LEFT OR RIGHT SIDE.

Sizes: 0-3 months (6-12 months, 2 years)
Finished Measurements:
Chest: approx. 19¾ (23¾, 27½) in / 50 (60, 70) cm
Length: approx. 11¾ (12¾, 13¾) in / 30 (32, 35) cm, as measured down from shoulders
Sleeve length: approx. 7 (8, 8¾) in / 18 (20, 22) cm, as measured straight out from underarm

Yarn: Fine Alpaca (Tynn Alpakka) from Du Store Alpakka (CYCA #1 [sock/fingering/baby], 100% alpaca, 183 yd/167 m / 50 g)
Yarn Amounts: 150 (150, 200) g of Color 1, Pink and 50 g (all sizes) of Color 2, Orange
Notions: 5 (6, 7) buttons
Crochet Hook: U.S. size E-4 / 3.5 mm
Gauge: 20 dc = 4 in / 10 cm. Adjust hook size to obtain correct gauge if necessary.

Begin at lower edge of back. Ch 52 (62, 72). Beginning in 4th ch from hook, work in dc across = 50 (60, 70) dc. Work back and forth in dc until piece measures approx. 7 (8, 8¾) in / 18 (20, 22) cm. Cut yarn and set piece aside.
Sleeves: Loosely ch 35 (40, 45). Attach to back with 1 dc in first dc. Continue with dc across back and end row with loosely ch 37 (42, 47). Turn, and, beginning in 4th ch from hook, work in dc across row = 120 (140, 160) dc total. Work 8 (10, 12) total rows for sleeves.

   Place a marker on each side of the center 16 (18, 20) sts of the row (= sts for back neck). Begin at outer edge of sleeve and work to first marker (= 52, 61, 70) dc; turn and sl st across first 5 (6, 7) sts. In the next st, ch 3 (= 1st dc). Continue in dc across row and then work 3 more rows in dc (all sizes), but, loosely ch 4 (all sizes) at the end of the 4th row (for front neck). Turn and, beginning in 4th ch from hook, work in dc across (= 2 dc added at center front). Work back in dc. Continue, loosely ch 18 (20, 22) for the rest of front neck at center front; turn. Be-

ginning in 4th ch from hook, work 3 (4, 5) rows in dc (sleeve ends here).
For size 6-12 months: Turn and work back and forth over the first 33 dc (front) until finished length.
For sizes 0–3 months and 2 years: Cut yarn, skip the first 35 (45) dc (sleeve sts) and then work back and forth over rem sts of front = 28 (33, 38) dc until finished length.

   Work opposite side of front as follows: Beginning at the 2nd marker, at back neck, ch 3 (= 1st dc), work in dc across row; turn and work back in dc until 5 (6, 7) sts rem. Turn and work 2 more rows in dc. Cut yarn, ch 2 and dc back; turn and work in dc across all sts of row (including the 2 ch at end for neck). *At the same time* as shaping front, make buttonholes (see details below), beginning on 2nd row of front. Cut yarn, ch 16 (18, 20) for rest of front neck and complete row in dc (= 1st row of front). Turn and work a total of 3 (4, 5) rows; sleeve ends here. Continue until front is finished length.

Buttonholes: If starting at center front, work 2 dc (1st dc = ch 3), ch 2, skip 2 dc, continue in dc across row. If beginning from the side, work until 4 dc rem, skip 2 dc, ch 2, work 2 dc. On the row following a buttonhole, work 2 dc around ch loop of buttonhole. Make a buttonhole on every 5th row until there are a total of 5 (6, 7) buttonholes.

Finishing
Weave in all ends on WS. Decide which side you want the buttonholes on and then seam sides and sleeves.
Crocheted edging: Begin at center of back neck with Color 2 and work in sc around all the edges of the cardigan. The neckline will be more rounded once you work the sc edging. Next, work a round of "small fans" (see Edging 6, page 142).

Baby cardigan

Short-Sleeved Tunic

THE TUNIC IS CROCHETED FROM THE BOTTOM UP IN TWO SECTIONS—
A FRONT AND A BACK.

Sizes: 1 (2) years
Finished Measurements:
Chest: 22 (24½) in / 56 (62) cm
Total length: approx. 15¾ (17¾) in / 40 (45) cm

Yarn: Alpaca from Drops (CYCA #2 [sport/baby], 100% alpaca, 182 yd/166 m / 50 g)
Yarn Amounts:
100 g of **Color 1:** Wine Red
50 g each of **Color 2:** Deep Rose and **Color 3:** Orange
50 g of **Color 4:** Rose [Fabel from Drops (CYCA #1 [sock/fingering/baby], 75% wool/25% nylon, 224 yd/205 m/50 g)]
Notions: 8 buttons approx. ⅜ in / 1 cm in diameter
Crochet Hook: U. S. size H-8 / 5 mm and U.S. size E-4 / 3.5 mm for finishing
Gauge: 14 dc with larger hook = 4 in / 10 cm. Adjust hook size to obtain correct gauge if necessary.

Tip

To avoid weaving in all the ends after the color changes later on, work as follows:
Ch 3 (= 1st dc) with the new color. Lay the old color beside the new color along top of previous row. Work 5–7 dc over both strands. Continue with new color only.

NOTE: Begin every row with ch 3 (= 1st dc). This is not repeated in the instructions below. Hold yarn doubled throughout.

FRONT

With Color 1 and larger hook, ch 52 (56).

Row 1: Beginning in 4th ch from hook, work 49 (53) dc = total of 50 (54) dc.

Row 2: Change to Color 2 and work dc across.

Row 3: Change to Color 3 and work dc across.

Row 4: Change to Color 4 and work dc across.

Row 5: Change to Color 1 and decrease 1 st at each side = 48 (52) sts rem. (For information on how to decrease, see page 150 in the Crochet School section).
Repeat Rows 2–5 until 40 (44) sts rem. Finish by working Rows 2–4 once more.

»—→

Continuing in color sequence, shape armholes by skipping the first 5 dc; ch 3 in next st, dc across until 5 sts rem = 30 (34) dc. Turn and work 1 sl st into 1st dc. Dc until 1 st rem = 28 (32) sts rem; turn. Decrease the same way on every row until 14 (14) sts rem. Set piece aside and make the back.

BACK

Work as for front to armhole shaping. Continuing in color sequence, ch 30 (30), work in dc across back—30 (34) dc—and then ch 30 (30); turn. Change colors and ch 3 + 1 dc in last ch for the color change (= 4th ch from hook). Work in dc over all the sts, with 2 dc in last st = 92 (96) dc. Turn and continue in dc but work 2 dc in the first and last st of each row. *At the same time*, decrease 8 sts evenly spaced across each row until 44 (48) sts rem. (See page 150, "Decreasing within the piece," in the Crochet School section.)

Finishing

Weave in any remaining ends that were not woven in as you worked. Place the front and back together with RS facing RS and seam from the bottom up to the underarms, using sc through both layers or sew together. Turn work right side out.

Edging around yoke: Begin at right side of front with larger hook: work 3 dc in the corner. Continue in dc around the neck, with 3 dc in each corner. With smaller size hook, finish with 1 rnd sc around neck with 1 sc in each dc. *At the same time*, decrease 2 sts evenly spaced across front. Work the same way around back neck, decreasing 8 sts evenly spaced across. The decreases will hold in the neckline.

Sew on 4 buttons on each side of the raglan shaping on back. Use the natural "holes" between the dc on the front as buttonholes.

Short-sleeved tunic

Green Hat

A SIMPLE HAT, CROCHETED FROM
THE BRIM UP. MAKE IT WITH OR
WITHOUT A POMPOM ON TOP.
[Design: Olaug Kleppe for Dale Garn AS]

Sizes: 2 (4, 6, 8) years

Yarn: Hegre from Dale Garn (CYCA #4 [worsted/afghan/aran], 100% wool, 82 yd/75 m / 50 g), 100 g Green
Crochet Hook: U.S. size MN-13 / 9 mm
Gauge: 8 sts in pattern = 4 in / 10 cm. Adjust hook size to obtain correct gauge if necessary.

Ch 32 (34, 36, 38) and join into a ring with 1 sl st into 1st ch. Ch 2 and then work 1 hdc in each ch around. Continue around with 1 hdc between each hdc of previous rnd. Do not begin rnd with ch 2 but work spiraling around. When hat measures 6¼ (6¾, 7, 7½) in / 16 (17, 18, 19) cm, work 1 sc (instead of hdc) between each hdc around and continue in sc. On the next rnd, skip every other st and then work 1 rnd without decreasing. Decrease, skipping every other st, and then work 1 rnd without decreasing. Cut yarn and bring end through last st. Tighten end and fasten off. Make a pompom about 2¾ in / 7 cm in diameter (see page 165 in the Crochet School section) and sew securely to top of hat.

Ladybug Bib

THIS PRACTICAL BIB CAN BE DECO-
RATED WITH MANY MOTIFS OTHER
THAN A LADY BUG. PERHAPS YOU'D
LIKE TO CHOOSE A FLOWER FROM
THE BOOK (SEE THE CROCHET
SCHOOL ON PAGE 143).

Yarn: Pt Petunia from Rauma (CYCA #3, 100% cotton, 120 yd/110 m / 50 g)
Yarn Amounts:
50 g White and small amounts of Red and Black
Crochet Hook: U.S. size D-3 / 3 mm
Measurements: Length, approx. 11¾ in / 30 cm; width, approx. 8 in / 20 cm at widest point

NOTE: Shrink the bib slightly by washing at 140°F / 60°C for the first wash.

Ch 63 a little tightly.

Row 1: Beginning in 4th ch from hook, work in dc across. Place a marker on every 10th st (= 5 markers).

Row 2: Ch 3 (= 1st dc); work 1 dc in each of next 9 sts. In the space between just worked dc and the next dc, work (1 dc, ch 1, 1 dc). Increase the same way at each marker = 10 sts increased.

Rows 3–4: Ch 3 (= 1st dc). Work in dc, increasing in the ch st at each marked st = total of 20 sts increased over the two rows. Cut yarn.

Row 5: Begin 1 dc before the ch loop at the 2nd marker from back neck—attach yarn with 1 sl st and ch 3 (= 1st dc). Continue to work in dc to the center front of the bib; increase 2 dc as before. Continue with 1 dc in each st until 1 dc past next ch loop.

Rows 6–18: Work in dc, increasing as for Row 5 on every row. Work as set until bib is desired length.

Edging: Work Edging 5 (see page 141) around outer edges of bib.

Ties (make 2 alike): With Red, chain a cord to desired length. Turn and work 1 sl st in each ch across. Attach a tie at each side of neck opening (see photo).

LADYBUG
With Red, chain and work 6 rnds in circular single crochet (see page 153 in Crochet School section). Make the back ridge by working slip stitches across the diameter. With Black, em-broider a little triangle for the "snout" and three cross stitches on each side for the spots. Sew the ladybug securely to the bib.

Ladybug bib

Beaded Bag

THIS FINE LITTLE BAG WILL PLEASE ANY-
ONE. IT'S ALSO EASY TO MAKE. IF YOU
NEED A BIRTHDAY GIFT IN A HURRY, GRAB
SOME COTTON YARNS FROM YOUR YARN
BASKET. IF THE YARN IS VERY FINE, HOLD
IT DOUBLED. YOU CAN ALSO MAKE THE
BAG STRIPED.

Yarn: Paris from Drops (CYCA #4 [worsted/afghan/aran],
100% cotton, 82 yd/75 m / 50 g), 100 g Pale Yellow
Notions: Wooden beads and other ornaments as you like
Crochet Hook: U.S. size G-6 / 4 mm
Measurements: 6 x 6 in / 15 x 15 cm (measured flat)

The bag is worked in hdc from the bottom up.

Loosely ch 21.

Row 1: Beginning in 3rd ch from hook, loosely work 1 sl st
into each ch around—make sure chain does not pull in.

Rnd 2: 1 sl st (center of short end), ch 2 (= 1 hdc), work 20
hdc on opposite side of foundation chain, 1 hdc (= center
of the other short end) and end with 20 hdc = total of 42
hdc.

Rnds 3–14: Spiral around with 1 hdc in each hdc (do not
ch at beg of rnd).

Rnd 15: Work as for Rnd 14, but decrease 2 hdc at each
short end by skipping 1 hdc 2 times, with 1 hdc between
skipped sts.

Rnd 16: Work in hdc to center of long side. Make a loop
for the decorative bead: Ch 13, insert hook into 10th ch
from hook and work 1 sl st, ch 3. Continue in hdc until
1 hdc past short side (that is, work in hdc over the long
side); turn, *ch 2 (= 1st hdc), 2 hdc; turn; rep from * over
the 3 hdc until strap measures approx. 19¾ in / 50 cm or
desired length. Attach strap to other short side.

Sew button to close with loop and decorate with wooden
beads.

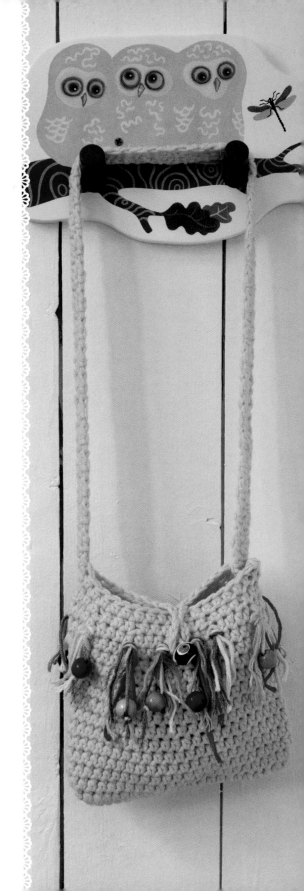

Giraffe

A CUTE TOY FOR THE YOUNGEST! WE DECIDED TO CROCHET IT
WITH A LIGHTER WEIGHT COTTON YARN SO THE GIRAFFE WOULD
BE MORE FLEXIBLE AND BECAUSE OF THE LONG NECK.

The heavier the yarn you use with the U.S. size C-2–D-3 / 2.5–3 mm hook, the firmer the giraffe will be. Maybe it will stand up on its own? However, this should be a comfy toy similar to a cloth doll. It will be what it will be! The giraffe is made in several sections that are joined afterwards. Read through the instructions completely before you start so they will be easier to understand. When the right side of the piece is shown, the neck will be on the right side and the rear on the left. We suggest that you crochet in the ends as you work so you won't have as much finishing to do.

Yarn: Pt Pandora from Rauma (CYCA #1 [sock/fingering/baby], 100% cotton, 180 yd/165 m / 50 g)
Yarn Amounts:
100 g **of Color 1:** Brown
50 g each of:
Color 2: Pink
Color 3: Lime
Color 4: Blue
Color 5: Mint
Color 6: Lacquer Red
Color 7: Purple
Color 8: Natural White
Notions: Foam rubber chunks or fiber fill, 2 eyes (use child-safe eyes or crochet on pupils with leftover yarn)
Crochet Hook: U.S. size C-2–D-3 / 2.5–3 mm

Gauge: 20 sc and 16 rows = approx. 2¾ x 2¾ in / 7 x 7 cm. Adjust hook size to obtain correct gauge if necessary.
Measurements: approx. 19¾ in / 50 cm tall as measured from the top of the head and straight down front legs.

Construction: The giraffe is worked back and forth in sc. Turn each row with ch 2 (= 1st sc)—this is not repeated in the instructions below. The color sequence is from Color 1–Color 8, with 2 rows of each color throughout except for the feet.

RIGHT BACK LEG (= only half the leg)
With Color 1, ch 16. Beginning in 2nd ch from hook, work 15 sc. Work a total of 4 rows. Change to Color 2 and work 14 rows in sc (changing colors after every 2 rows); end with Color 8. On the next row (Color 1), increase 2 sts at the right side by working 3 sc into the 1st st.

RIGHT FRONT LEG
Work as for right back leg but increase 2 sts at the end of the row (on the left side). Next, ch 12 and join to back leg with 1 sl st. Cut yarn.

BODY (as seen from right side)
The body is crocheted over the two parts of the leg. Begin at left side (with 1st row of Color 1) and work a total of 7 rows in sc over the 46

»——→

sts, changing colors in sequence. Now work 2 rows over the first 30 sts on the right side of the piece, and then 6 rows over 46 sts.

Shape left side as follows: On every other row, at left side, decrease 3 sts two times, 6 sts three times, and 2 sts three times (= 16 sts rem or neck). Work 20 more rows in sc.

On the next row, increase 1 st on the right side and decrease 1 st at left side. When there are 60 rows on the neck, ch 14 at the right side for the top of the head. Beginning in 2nd ch from hook, work 13 sc in addition to the 16 sc already on row. Now decrease 1 st at each side on every other row 4 times, and on the next row, decrease 2 sts at each side (= 17 sts rem).

Turn work and make the snout (muzzle) over the 13 sts you began crocheting at the top of the head. *At the same time*, increase 1 st at outer edge on the next 6 rows. Also *at the same time*, decrease 1 st at inner edge (at neck). On the following 4 rows, decrease 1 st at each side= 5 sts rem.

Make the other half of the giraffe the same way, reversing shaping.

BELLY

Make two more legs as before and join them with 12 ch. Work 10 rows over all the sts, *at the same time* increasing 1 st each in the first and last st of each row. On the next 10 rows, decrease 1 st at beginning and end of each row. Join the two legs over the first and last 17 sts.

SMALL AND LARGE BROWN SPOTS

Make a magic ring (see page 147) and work 8 sc around ring; join with 1 sl st into 1st sc. Pull together. For the large spots, work another rnd with 2 sc in each st = 16 sc around.

SOLES (make 4)

Work as for large spots but, on the 3rd rnd, increase to 24 sc and, on the 4th rnd, increase to 30 sc.

EYES

Use Color 4. Work as for large spots but, on the 2nd rnd, work 2 sc in each of the first 4 sts and then work the last 4 sts as: 2 hdc in next sc, 1 dc + 1 tr in next sc, 1 tr + 1 dc in next sc, 2 hdc in last sc. You can make the pupils as for the small brown spots or embroider them on the eyes.

EARS

With Color 1, ch 2 and work 2 sc into 1st ch. On each of the next 5 rows, increase 1 st at each side by working 2 sc in each of the edge sts. Work 5 rows, decreasing 1 st at each side by turning 1 st before the last st on each row.

Finishing

Sew the brown spots and eyes on by hand with fine stitches. Seam the legs on the two outer sections. Seam the body under the belly. Sew on all the soles securely. Fill the legs well with foam rubber chunks or fiber fill. Fold in the two triangular pieces on each side of the belly. Seam center front and along the head. Fill the head and muzzle. Seam the neck and fill. Finally, fill the body and seam together along the back. Make a tassel for the tail with brown yarn and sew it securely to the back. Sew the ears to the head.

Mane: With Color 1, work sc from the top of the forehead and back down the neck. With three strands of yarn held together for each bundle, tie yarn into each sc down the neck. Alternately, you can use loop crochet (see page 157). Trim mane evenly.

1970s Stripes

HERE'S A COLORFUL PATTERN THAT
WORKS JUST AS WELL FOR A BABY
BLANKET AS FOR A BRIGHT KITCHEN
TOWEL. THE PATTERN WILL ALSO
LOOK NICE IN A SINGLE COLOR FOR
A COVERLET.

Yarn: Mandarin Petit from SandnesGarn (CYCA #1
[sock/fingering/baby], 100% cotton, 195 yd/178 m / 50 g)
Yarn Amounts: 50 g White and 100 g each of: Orange,
Lime, Blue, Pink, and Light Purple
Crochet Hook: U.S. size D-3 / 3 mm
Measurements: approx. 19¾ x 25½ in / 50 x 65 cm

With Pink, ch 123.

Row 1: Begin in 5th ch from hook (= 1 dc + 2 ch). Work in
dc groups as follows: *(2 dc, ch 1, 2 dc) in same st, skip 2
ch, 1 dc, skip 2 ch; rep from * across and end with 1 dc.

Row 2: Ch 3 (= 1st dc), *(2 dc, ch 1, 2 dc) in ch loop, 1 dc
in dc between dc groups; rep from * across and end with
1 dc.

Rows 3–60: Work as for Row 2 in the following color
sequence:

5 rows Pink	5 rows Orange
1 row White	1 row White
3 rows Blue	5 rows Purple
4 rows Lime	3 rows Pink
1 row White	3 rows Blue
3 rows Orange	4 rows Lime
5 rows Purple	1 row White
1 row White	5 rows Orange
5 rows Pink	
3 rows Blue	Cut yarn and weave in all
1 row White	ends on WS.
3 rows Lime	

Puff Sleeve Sweater

THIS IS AN EASY SWEATER THAT EVEN A BEGINNER CAN MAKE. THE PUFF SLEEVES ADD A FEMININE STYLING. THE KNITTED RIBBING ON THE SLEEVES IS WORKED LAST SO YOU CAN ADJUST THE LENGTH AS NECESSARY.

Sizes: S (M, L)

Finished Measurements:

Chest: approx. 34¾ (39½, 44½) in / 88 (100, 113) cm

Total length: approx. 25½ (26½, 27¼) in/ 65 (67, 69) cm

Yarn: Hubro from Dale Garn (CYCA #6 [bulky/ roving], 100% wool, 72 yd/66 m / 100 g), 1000 (1100, 1100) g Green

Crochet Hook: U.S. size L-11 or MN-13 / 8 or 9 mm

Knitting Needles: U.S. size 11 / 8 mm: set of 4 or 5 dpn

Gauge: 8 sc = 4 in / 10 cm. Adjust hook size to obtain correct gauge if necessary.

Garment Construction: The body is crocheted around with sts through back loops only to the underarms. The piece is then divided and new sts chained for the sleeves. The front and back are worked separately, with alternate rows through back and front loops (see page 155 in the Crochet School section). The sweater is crocheted rather loosely—check your gauge and adjust hook size as necessary.

Ch 70 (80, 90) and join into a ring with 1 sl st into 1st ch.

Rnd 1: Begin with ch 1 (= 1st sc) and then work in sc through back loop around, ending with 1 sl st into 1st ch.

Repeat Rnd 1 until piece measures 17¾ (18½, 19¼) in / 45 (47, 49) cm. Divide body for front and back; cut yarn.

BACK

CO 30 (30, 35) for one sleeve and then sc 35 (40, 45) in back loops across back. Ch 31 (31, 36) for opposite sleeve; turn. Beginning in 2nd ch from hook, work 30 (30, 35) sc. Work across back with sc in front loops; turn and work sc through back loops across. Continue alternating rows through front and back loops until approx. 8 (8¼, 8¾) in / 20 (21, 22) cm from foundation of chain of sleeve.

FRONT

Don't forget to alternate rows through front/ back loops.

Work as for back until 4 in / 10 cm from sleeve foundation chain. Pm on each side of the 11 center sts (all sizes).

Shape neck: Work to 1st marker; turn and work back; turn. *Work until 1 st before previous turn; turn and work back. Rep from * once more. Continue working back and forth over all rem sts to total length. Work the same way on opposite side, reversing shaping.

Finishing

Seam shoulders and down sleeves. Seam underarms. Begin at center back neck and work in sc around neckline.

KNITTED RIBBING FOR SLEEVES

With dpn, pick up and knit 40 (42, 46) sts around end of sleeve; divide sts onto dpn and join. Knit 1 rnd, decreasing to 28 sts (all sizes). Work in k2, p2 ribbing for desired length. Cut yarn and weave in all ends on WS.

Round Yoke Cardigan

THIS FEMININE AND PRETTY YOKED CARDIGAN IS EASY TO MAKE AND TO VARY. THE CARDIGAN IS WORKED FROM THE TOP DOWN. THE SLEEVES ARE CROCHETED AND THEN THE FRONTS. BY WORKING FROM THE TOP DOWN, YOU CAN OMIT THE SLEEVES FOR A VEST OR MAKE SHORT SLEEVES. A SHORT CARDIGAN CAN BECOME A PRETTY BOLERO, WITH OR WITHOUT SLEEVES. ALL YOU HAVE TO DO IS CHOOSE!

Size: M

Finished Measurements:

Chest: 36¼ in / 92 cm (when buttoned at the front)

Total length: 23¾ in / 60 cm (or desired length)

Sleeve length: 19 in / 48 cm

Yarn: Lille Lerke from Dale Garn (CYCA #1 [sock/fingering/baby], 53% Merino wool/47% cotton, 155 yd/142 m / 50 g), 450 g White + Kid Silk from Drops (CYCA #0 [lace/fingering], 75% Mohair, 25% silk, 218 yd/199 m / 25 g), 175 g Natural

Notions: 7 butttons

Crochet Hook: U.S. size 7 / 4.5 mm

Gauge: 17 sc with 1 strand of each yarn held together = 4 in / 10 cm.

Adjust hook size to obtain correct gauge if necessary.

To make a smaller size, substitute a finer yarn for the Lille Lerke (for example, a 100% baby wool instead) and use a hook 1 U.S. size or .5 mm smaller. For a larger size, do the opposite (substitute Lerke from Dale Garn). In either case, it is important to use the fine mohair/silk yarn. Make a gauge swatch. If you have 1 st more in 4 in / 10 cm (18 sc = 4 in / 10 cm), the cardigan will be about 2 in / 5 cm narrower, and, if there is 1 st less in 4 in / 10 cm (16 sc = 4 in / 10 cm), the cardigan will be about 2 in / 5 cm wider.

Pattern: Crossed Double Crochet

*Skip the 1st st, work 1 dc in the 2nd st, work 1 dc in the 1st st; rep from *.

The rows worked in sc begin with ch 1 (= 1st sc)—this information is not repeated in the instructions below.

NOTE: Work with a strand of each yarn held together throughout.

Ch 121.

Row 1: Beginning in 2nd ch from hook, work in sc across = 120 sc.

Row 2: Ch 1 (= 1st sc), sc, increasing 12 sts evenly spaced across = 132 sc. (See page 148, "Increasing stitches," in the Crochet School section.)

≫⟶

Row 3: Ch 3 = 1 dc, work in crossed double crochet until 1 st rem, 1 dc in last st = 132 dc.

Row 4: Work as for Row 3.

Row 5: Ch 1 (= 1st sc), sc, increasing 12 sts evenly spaced across = 144 sc.

Row 6: Sc across.

Rows 7–9: Ch 3 (= 1st dc), work in crossed double crochet as for Row 3, ending with 1 dc in last st = 144 dc.

Row 10: Sc, increasing 14 sts evenly spaced across = 158 sc.

Row 11: Sc across.

Rows 12–15: Ch 3 (= 1st dc), work in crossed double crochet as for Row 3, ending with 1 dc in last st = 158 dc.

Row 16: Ch 1 (= 1st sc), sc, increasing 12 sts evenly spaced across = 170 sc.

Row 17: Sc across.

Rows 18–23: Ch 3 (= 1st dc), work in crossed double crochet as for Row 3, ending with 1 dc in last st = 170 dc.

Row 24: Ch 1 (= 1st sc), sc, increasing 30 sts evenly spaced across = 200 sc.

Now divide for the armholes at each side. Work down for the front and back; the sleeves will be worked later.

Row 25: Sc 30 (front), ch 10 (underarm), skip 35 sts, sc 70 (back), ch 10 (underarm), sc 30 (front).

Row 26: Sc 30 for front, 10 sc across underarm, 70 sc on back, 10 sc along underarm, 30 sc on front = 150 sts total. Pm at each side between the 5th and 6th underarm sts.

Rows 27–30: Sc across.
On the next row and every following 10th row, increase 2 sts at each side (= 4 new sts per row).

Row 31: Sc 34, 2 sc in each of the next 2 sc, 78 sc, 2 sc in each of next 2 sc, sc to end of row = 154 sc.

Rows 32–39: Sc across.

Row 40: Work as for Row 31 but work as: 35 sc, 2 sc in each of next 2 sc, 80 sc, 2 sc in each of next 2 sc, sc to end of row =158 sc.

Continue increasing 2 sts at each side on every 10th row until cardigan is desired length or 13½ in / 34 cm as measured from underarm = 4 increase rows for a total 174 sts.

SLEEVES (make both alike)
Beginning at center of underarm, work 50 sc around armhole. Beginning every row with ch 1 (= 1st sc), work back and forth in sc for 5½ in / 14 cm.

On each of the next 2 rows, decrease by working until 1 st rem; turn = 48 sts rem. *Work in sc for 2¾ in / 7 cm; decrease as before on the next 2 rows = 46 sts rem. Rep from * twice more = 42 sts rem. Continue without further shaping until sleeve is 15½ in / 39 cm long. Finish with 7 rows crossed double crochet or to desired length.

Tip
For a tighter neckline, before working the edging, work a row of sc around *at the same time* as you decrease about 15-20 sts evenly spaced. If that is not enough, work another decrease row.

FRONT BANDS
Left band: Beginning at top, work 90 sc down; turn and work back and forth in sc for a total of 5 rows.
Right band: Work as for left band, but make buttonholes on the 3rd row: Work 2 sc at top of band, ch 2, skip 2 sc, *10 sc, ch 2, skip 2 sc; rep from * until you have a total of 7 buttonholes. Finish row in sc; turn and work the last 2 rows, with 2 sc in each buttonhole loop.

Weave in all ends neatly on WS; sew on buttons.

Seed Stitch Crochet Vest

AN ELEGANT VEST WITH THE BACK AND FRONT WORKED SEPARATELY.
THE SLEEVES ARE CROCHETED ON AFTER SEAMING THE BODY.

Size: One size
Finished Measurements:
Chest: approx. 39½ in / 100 cm
Length: 23¾ in / 60 cm or desired length
Sleeve length: 7 in / 18 cm
Collar length: approx. 8¾ in / 22 cm

Yarn: Lima from Drops (CYCA #3 [DK/light worsted], 65% wool/35% alpaca, 98 yd/90 m / 50 g), 750 g Light Brown
Notions: 5 buttons
Crochet Hook: U.S. size J-10 or K-10½ / 6 or 7 mm (depending on how tightly you crochet) and U.S. size 7 / 4.5 mm for the edgings
Gauge: 18 sts x 18 rows on larger hook = 4 x 4 in / 10 x 10 cm.
Adjust hook size to obtain correct gauge if necessary.

BACK

Ch 91 with hook to give you correct gauge.

Row 1: Beginning in 3rd ch from hook, work in pattern: *1 sc, ch 1, skip 1 st; rep from * across and end with 1 sc, ch 2.

Row 2: Begin pattern in space between 1st and 2nd sc and continue as for Row 1, with sc and ch between sc and ch of previous row. End row as for Row 1.

Repeat Row 2 until piece measures 22½ in / 57 cm or desired length.

FRONT

Work as for back until front is 9 rows shorter than finished length.
Neckline: Pm at each side of the 30 center sts on front and work as follows: Beginning on one side, work in pattern to the first marker; turn and work back. Turn and work until 2 sts before previous turn; turn and work back. Turn and work until 2 st before previous turn; turn and work back. Turn and work a complete row; turn and work back; turn and work back. Cut yarn. Work the opposite of front neck the same way, reversing shaping.
Seam shoulders: Seam the sides until about 9¾ in / 25 cm from shoulder seam.
Lower edge of body: With smaller size hook for bands, make a band about 2 in / 5 cm wide, working in the round: Attach yarn with 1 sl st, (1 sc, ch 1, skip 1 st; rep from * around. Continue with sc and ch between previous sc and ch for 2 in / 5 cm without making an extra ch when starting a new round.

≫⟶

SLEEVES (make both alike)

With larger size hook, attach yarn with 1 sl st at lower end of armhole at one side. Work 92 sts in pattern around the armhole until sleeve is 5¼ in / 13 cm long. With smaller size hook for bands, work a band as for lower edge of body.

COLLAR

With larger size hook, attach yarn with 1 sl st at right shoulder (as viewed from back). Begin with ch 2 and then work in pattern as for body along the back and front. Turn with ch 3. Beginning in 3ʳᵈ ch from hook, continue in pattern around to the opposite side (also over the 2 ch) = approx. 110 sts around neck, end with ch 2. Turn and continue working back and forth. Every approx. 1½ in / 4 cm, make a buttonhole on the short side of the collar after turning: work 1 sc + 1 ch, skip 1 st,1 sc, ch 3, skip 2 sts (= 1 sc, ch 1), work in pattern to end of row. Turn and work back, with 1 sc, ch 1 over the 3 ch of the buttonhole; complete row. After last buttonhole row, work 3 more rows; cut yarn and fasten off.

Finishing

Weave in all ends neatly on WS. Sew on buttons.

Lace Pattern Cardigan

A DRESSY CARDIGAN IN A SPORTY COLOR. [Design: DROPS Design]

Sizes: S (M, L, XL)

Finished Measurements:

Chest: 33 (36¼, 40¼, 43¼) in / 84 (92, 102, 110) cm

Circumference at hip: 42½ (45¾, 49¾, 55) in / 108 (116, 126, 140) cm

Total length: 30 (30¾, 33, 34) in / 76 (78, 84, 86) cm

Sleeve length: 22½ in / 57 cm (all sizes)

Yarn: Karisma from Drops (CYCA #3 [DK/light worsted], 100% wool, 120 yd/110 m / 50 g), 700 (750, 850, 900) g of Mustard

Notions: 6 buttons about ¾ in / 20 mm diameter

Crochet Hook: U.S. size 7 / 4.5 mm

Gauge: 17 sts x 6 rows in pattern A.4 = 4 x 4 in / 10 x 10 cm.

Adjust hook size to obtain correct gauge if necessary.

Stitches and Patterns

1 bobble with 5 tr: Work 1 tr in next sc but do not bring yarn through last step (= 2 loops on hook). Work 1 tr in each of the next 4 sc the same way and end with yoh and through all 6 loops on hook.

1 bobble with 4 tr: Work 1 tr in next sc but do not bring yarn through last step (= 2 loops on hook). Work 1 tr in each of the next 3 sc the same way and end with yoh and through all 5 loops on hook.

1 bobble with 3 tr: Work 1 tr in next sc but do not bring yarn through last step (= 2 loops on hook). Work 1 tr in each of the next 2 sc the same way and end with yoh and through all 4 loops on hook.

Pattern A.1 (multiple of 6 sts + 1):

Row 1 (RS): Ch 4 (= 1st tr) in 1st sc, and continue with *ch 2, 1 bobble with 5 tr, ch 2, 1 tr in next sc; rep from * across.

Row 2 (WS): Ch 1, 3 sc in ch loop, 1 sc in next bobble, 2 sc in next ch loop, continue as follows: *1 sc in next tr, 2 sc in next ch loop, 1 sc in next bobble, 2 sc in next ch loop, 1 sc in next bobble, 2 sc in next ch loop; rep from * across, ending with 1 sc in the last ch loop of the row (= same number of sc as previously).

Pattern A.2 (multiple of 5 sts + 1):

Row 1 (RS): Ch 4 (= 1st tr) in 1st sc, and continue with *ch 2, 1 bobble with 4 tr, ch 2, 1 tr in next sc; rep from * across.

Row 2 (WS): Ch 1, 3 sc in ch loop, skip 1 bobble, 2 sc in next ch loop, continue as follows: *1 sc in next tr, 2 sc in next ch loop, skip next bobble, 2

≫⟶

Lace pattern cardigan

sc in next ch loop, skip next bobble, 2 sc in next ch loop; rep from * across, ending with 1 sc in the last ch loop of the row (= same number of sc as previously).

Pattern A.3 (multiple of 4 sts + 1):

Row 1 (RS): Ch 4 (= 1st tr) in 1st sc, and continue with *ch 1, 1 bobble with 3 tr, ch 1, 1 tr in next sc; rep from * across.

Row 2 (WS): Ch 1, 2 sc in 1st ch loop, 1 sc in next bobble, 1 sc in next ch loop, continue as follows: *1 sc in next tr, 1 sc in next ch loop, 1 sc in next bobble, 1 sc in next ch loop; rep from * across, ending with 1 sc in the last ch loop of the row (= same number of sc as previously).

Pattern A.4:

Row 1 (RS): Work across in dc.

Row 2 (WS): Work across in sc.

Increases: Increase 1 st by working 2 sts in the same st.

Dc rows: All of the dc rows are worked on the RS. Each dc row begins with ch 3 (= 1st dc), skip 1st sc of previous row and then work 1 dc in each sc across; turn.

Decreasing dc: Work 2 dc together as follows: work 1 dc in sc below but do not bring yarn through for last step (= 2 loops rem on hook). 1 dc in next sc, but, when ready to bring yarn through on last step, bring it through all 3 loops on hook = 1 dc decreased.
Decrease 3 dc at beginning or end of row by working the first or last 6 dc together, 2 x 2 x 2. Decrease 2 dc at beginning or end of row by working the first or last 4 dc together, 2 x 2. Decrease 1 dc at beginning or end of row by working the first or last 2 dc together.

Decreasing sc: Insert hook into st below and bring yarn through, hook into next st and yarn through; yoh and through all 3 loops on hook = 1 sc decreased.

Loosely ch 188 (200, 218, 242).

Beginning in 2nd ch from hook, work in sc across = 187 (199, 217, 241) sc.
 Turn (the 1st row = WS). Work 4 rows in sc, beginning each row with ch 1 (does not count as 1st sc).
 Now work Pattern A.1 [= 31 (33, 36, 40) repeats + 1 dtr]. After completing 2nd row, there should be 187 (199, 217, 241) sc across. Work Pattern A.1 a total of 6 (6, 7, 7) times, with the last sc row, on WS, as follows: Ch 1, 3 sc in 1st ch loop, skip 1st bobble, 2 sc in next ch loop,*1 sc in next tr, 2 sc in next ch loop, skip next bobble, 2 sc in next ch loop; rep from * across, ending with 3 sc in last ch loop = 156 (166, 181, 201) sc.
 Work Pattern A.2. After completing 2nd row, there should be 156 (166, 181, 201) sc across. Work Pattern A.2 a total of 6 times, with the last sc row, on WS, as follows: Ch 1, 2 sc in 1st ch loop, 1 sc in next bobble, 1 sc in next ch loop, *1 sc in next tr, 1 sc in next ch loop, 1 sc in next bobble, 1 sc in next ch loop; rep from * across, ending with 2 sc in last ch loop = 125 (133, 145, 161) sc.
 Now work Pattern A.3. After completing 2nd row, there should be 125 (133, 145, 161) sc across. Work Pattern A.3 a total of 6 times, and, on the last sc (WS) row, increase 10 (12, 14, 16) sc evenly spaced across = 135 (145, 159, 177) sc. The piece should now measure approx. 19 (19, 19¾, 19¾) in / 48 (48, 50.5, 50.5) cm.
 Continue with Pattern A.4 once. *At the same time* as working sc row on WS, increase 9 (11, 13, 11) sts evenly spaced across = 144 (156, 172, 188) sc. Work Pattern A.4 a total of 6 (7, 7, 8)

»——→

Lace pattern cardigan

times with the last sc row on WS. The piece should now measure approx. 22¾ (23¾, 24½, 24¾) in/ 58 (60, 62, 63) cm.

Do not cut yarn. Work front and back separately. Pm on each front 36 (39, 43, 47) sc in from each side on the last sc row = 72 (78, 86, 94) sc between markers on back.

RIGHT FRONT
Continue in Pattern A.4, and, *at the same time*, shape armhole on next RS row: work in dc until 3 sc rem before marker = 33 (36, 40, 44) dc. Turn = skip 3 sts before marker) and work in sc across WS.

Continue shaping armhole on every RS row: decrease 3 dc 0 (0,1, 1) times, decrease 2 dc 1 (1, 1, 3) times, and 1 dc 1 (3, 3, 2) times.

At the same time, after completing pattern A.4 a total of 5 (6, 6, 6) times (as counted from marker on last sc row before armhole shaping), shape neck on the next dc row on RS: Cut yarn. Ch 3 (= 1st dc) in the 7th (7th, 8th, 8th) sc from center front= skip 6 (6, 7, 7) dc from center front. *At the same time*, continue armhole shaping at the end of the row if not already completed. Turn and work 1 sc row on WS.

Next, decrease at beginning of every RS row as follows: decrease 2 dc 2 times and 1 dc 2 times. After completing all the decreases, 18 (19, 19, 20) sts rem for shoulder.

Work Pattern A.4 a total of 11 (12, 13, 13) times (as counted from the marker in the last sc row before armhole shaping). The piece should now measure approx. 30 (31½, 33, 33½) in / 76 (80, 84, 85) cm. End with a sc row. Cut yarn and fasten off.

LEFT FRONT
Continue with Pattern A.4 *at the same time* as shaping armhole, beginning on next RS row: Skip the first 3 dc from marker at side, ch 3 (= 1st dc) in next sc = 4th sc from marker; complete row in dc = 33 (36, 40, 44) dc. Turn and work in sc across WS.

Continue shaping armhole on every RS row: decrease 3 dc 0 (0,1, 1) times, decrease 2 dc 1 (1, 1, 3) times, and 1 dc 1 (3, 3, 2) times.

At the same time, after completing Pattern A.4 a total of 5 (6, 6, 6) times (as counted from marker on last sc row before armhole shaping), shape neck on the next dc row on RS: Work in dc until skip 6 (6, 7, 7) dc from center front; turn and work sc across on WS. *At the same time*, continue armhole shaping at beginning of the row if not already completed.

Next, decrease at end of every RS row as follows: decrease 2 dc 2 times and 1 dc 2 times. After completing all the decreases, 18 (19, 19, 20) sts rem for shoulder.

Work Pattern A.4 a total of 11 (12, 13, 13) times (as counted from the marker in the last sc row before armhole shaping). The piece should now measure approx. 30 (31½, 33, 33½) in / 76 (80, 84, 85) cm. End with a sc row. Cut yarn and fasten off.

BACK
Continue with Pattern A.4 *at the same time* as shaping armholes, beginning on next RS row: Skip the first 3 dc from marker at side, ch 3 (= 1st dc) in next sc = 4th sc from marker; 1 dc in each sc until 3 sc rem = 66 (72, 80, 88) dc. Turn (= skip 3 sc) and work in sc across WS.

»—→

Continue shaping armholes at beginning and end of every RS row: decrease 3 dc 0 (0,1, 1) times, decrease 2 dc 1 (1, 1, 3) times, and 1 dc 1 (3, 3, 2) times = 60 (62, 64, 66) sts rem.

Work Pattern A.4 a total of 9 (10, 11, 11) times (as counted from the marker in the last sc row before armhole shaping).

RIGHT SHOULDER
Work 19 (20, 20, 21) dc on RS. Turn and work 19 (20, 20, 21) sc on WS; turn. On the next row, decrease 1 dc at end of row for back neck = 18 (19, 19, 20) sts rem for shoulder. Work 1 sc row on WS [= a total of 11 (12, 13, 13) rep of Pattern A.4 as counted from the last sc row before armhole shaping]. Cut yarn and fasten off. The piece should now measure approx. 30 (31½, 33, 33½) in / 76 (80, 84, 85) cm.

LEFT SHOULDER
Work on RS, beginning at neck: count out 19 (20, 20, 21) sts in from left side and begin with

ch 3 in that sc. Work 1 dc in each of next 18 (19, 19, 20) sts. Do not work over the center 22 (22, 24, 24) sts for the neck. Turn and work 1 sc in each dc across; turn. On the next row (dc), decrease 1 dc at beginning of row for neck = 18 (19, 19, 20) sts rem for shoulder. Work 1 sc row on WS. Cut yarn and fasten off. The piece should now measure approx. 30 (31½, 33, 33½) in / 76 (80, 84, 85) cm.

SLEEVES (make both alike)
Loosely ch 37 (37, 42, 42). Turn and work 1 sc in 2nd ch from hook and then 1 sc in each ch across = 36 (36, 41, 41) sc. Turn (1st row = WS). Work 4 more sc rows (= a total of 5 sc rows). The sleeve should now measure approx. 1 in / 2.5 cm.

Continue in Pattern A.2 [= 7 (7, 8, 8) rep across + 1 tr]. After completing 2nd row, there should be 36 (36, 41, 41) sc across.
Work Pattern A.2 a total of 3 times. On the last sc row on WS, increase 0 (4, 2, 4) sc evenly

Lace pattern cardigan

spaced across = 36 (40, 43, 45) sc. The sleeve should now measure approx. 4 in / 10 cm. Continue in Pattern A.4 until sleeve is finished length, and, *at the same time*, increase 1 dc in the outermost sc at each side on the 1st dc row (= 2 dc increased). Increase the same way at each side on every other dc row (= every 4th row) a total of 8 (8, 8, 8) more times = 54 (58, 61, 63) sts. Work Pattern A.4 a total of 21 (21, 20, 20) times (the last row is a sc row on WS). The sleeve should now measure approx. 17¾ (17¾, 17, 17) in / 45 (45, 43.5, 43.5) cm. The shorter length for the larger sizes takes into account the longer sleeve top and wider shoulder.

Shape the sleeve cap on the next dc row on RS: Sl st to 4th sc, ch 3 in same sc (= 1st dc), 1 dc in each sc until 3 sc rem on row = 48 (52, 55, 57) dc. Turn and work sc row on WS. Continue shaping sleeve cap at each side on every RS row as follows: Decrease 3 dc 1 (2, 2, 2) times, 2 dc 2 (2, 2, 3) times, 1 dc 1 (0, 1, 1) time, 2 dc 2 (2, 2, 1) times. On next RS row, decrease 3 dc at each side = 18 (18, 19, 21) sts rem. On next WS row, decrease 3 sc at each side = 12 (12, 13, 15) sts rem. Cut yarn and fasten off. The sleeve should now measure approx. 22½ in / 57 cm (all sizes).

Make the other sleeve the same way.

TAB

This piece is worked in the round. Loosely ch 19 with hook U.S. size 7 / 4.5 mm; turn and work 3 sc in the 2nd ch from hook and then 1 sc in each ch until 1 ch rem. Work 3 sc in last ch; turn and continue with 1 sc in each ch on opposite side of foundation chain. (See page 153, "Crocheting in the round," in the Crochet School section.)

On the next rnd, work 1 sc in each sc, but, on each short end, increase 1 sc by working 2 sc in same st in each of the center 3 sc = 3 sc increased at each short end. Continue around, increasing

in each short side the same way until tab measures approx. 5½ (5½, 6, 6) in / 14 (14, 15, 15) cm in width. Work 1 sl st into next sc, cut yarn and fasten off.

Finishing

Seam shoulders with fine stitches in the outermost st loops. Attach sleeves and seam sleeves.

Place tab at the center of the back where pattern A.3 shifts to A.4. Sew a button to each side of tab, sewing through both layers.

COLLAR

Begin on RS at top of right front. Work 80-100 sc along neck edge. Work 1 sc row on WS, adjusting stitch count to 80 (82, 84, 88) sc. Work 4 more rows in sc = a total of 6 sc rows. On the next row, increase 3 sc evenly spaced across = 83 (85, 87, 91) sc. Continue working in sc until there are a total of 11 sc rows. On the next sc row, increase 3 (6, 4, 5) sc evenly spaced across = 86 (91, 91, 96) sc. Now work 1 rep of Pattern A.2 = 17 (18, 18, 19) rep + 1 tr. Work 2 more rows of sc. Cut yarn and fasten off. The collar should measure approx. 3½ in / 9 cm.

BUTTON AND BUTTONHOLE BANDS

With RS facing, work 130-150 sc along right front (including short side of collar). Work 1 row of sc on WS, adjusting stitch count to 128 (134, 138, 140) sc. On the next row (RS), work in sc until 80 (84, 84, 84) sc rem (from lower edge), *ch 2, skip 2 sc, work 13 (14, 16, 17) sc; rep from * once more, ch 2, skip 2 sc, work 12 sc, ch 2, skip 2 sc, work the last 2 sc on row (= 4 buttonholes); turn. Work 2 sc rows, with 2 sc in each ch loop. Cut yarn and fasten off = 5 sc rows total.

Work the button band on left front the same way, omitting buttonholes. Sew 4 buttons to left band, spaced as for buttonholes.

Lace pattern cardigan

Lace Collars

LACE COLLARS ARE BACK IN STYLE.

These collars were inspired by those in style between the 1940s and 1960s. At that time, most collars were made with fabric edged with lace, either ready- or hand-made. However, many women liked to crochet the entire collar as we have done here. As a general rule, cotton crochet thread was used but we decided to try an alpaca and silk yarn for one collar and a blend of alpaca, silk, and cotton for the other.

Size: Women's
Measurements: Both collars measure 19¾–20½ in / 50–52 cm long as measured along top edge at neck.

Yarn:
Collar A: Baby Alpaca Silk from Drops (CYCA #2 [sport/baby], 70% alpaca/30% silk, 183 yd/167 m / 50 g): 50 g each of Color 1: Light Sea Green and Color 2: Brown
Collar B: Baby Alpaca Silk from Drops: 50 g of Color 1: Green and Vipe from Dale Garn (CYCA #2 [sport/baby], 100% cotton, 137 yd/125 m / 50 g), 50 g of Color 2: Corn Yellow
Notions: A small button for Collar A.
Crochet Hook: U.S. size C-2 / 2.5 mm

Collar A

With Color 1, ch 8 and join into a ring with 1 sl st into 1st ch; turn.

Row 1: Ch 3, 12 dc around ring; turn.

Row 2: Ch 4, 1 dc in 2nd dc, *ch 1, 1 dc in next dc; rep from * 9 times and end with ch 1, 1 dc in 3rd ch = 13 dc; turn.

Row 3: Ch 5, 1 dc in 2nd dc, *ch 2, 1 dc in next dc; rep from * 9 times and end with ch 2, 1 dc in 3rd of the 4 ch = 13 dc; turn.

Row 4: Ch 5, 1 dc in 2nd dc, *ch 3, 1 dc in next dc; rep from * 9 times and end with ch 3, 1 dc in 3rd of the 5 ch = 13 dc; turn.

Row 5: Work (1 sc, 3 dc, 1 sc) in each ch loop = 12 groups; turn and ch 8; turn, 1 sl st into 2nd dc of the 3 dc at end of Row 5; turn.

Row 6: Ch 3, 8 dc in ch-8 loop (= 9 dc); turn.

Row 7: Ch 4, 1 dc in 2nd dc, *ch 1, 1 dc in next dc; rep from * 5 times and end with ch 1, 1 dc in the 3rd ch, 1 sl st into 2nd dc of next group on the 5th row = 9 dc; turn.

Row 8: Ch 5, skip 1st dc, 1 dc in 2nd dc, *ch 2, 1 dc in next st; rep from * 5 times and end with ch 2, 1 dc in the 3rd of the 4 ch = 9 dc; turn.

Row 9: Ch 6, 1 dc in 2nd dc, *ch 3, 1 dc in next dc; rep from * 5 times and end with ch 3, 1 dc in the 3rd of the 5 ch, 1 sl st into 2nd dc of next group on 5th row = 9 dc; turn.

Row 10: (1 sc, 3 dc, 1 sc) in every ch-3 loop = 8 dc groups, ch 8; turn with 1 sl st into the 2nd of the 3 dc at end of Row 9; turn.

Repeat Rows 6–10 until collar has 4 fans on the left side of the center "complete" fan. On the 4th fan, do not ch 8 all the way to the end. Cut yarn and pull end through last st. Continue on

»⟶

the opposite side of the "complete" fan, beginning at outermost edge of right side, above the first sc. Ch 8, 1 sl st into 2nd dc of the 3 dc to the left; turn. Repeat Rows 6–10 until there are 4 fans on this side.

Change to Color 2 and begin at one end: work 90 sc along the top edge of the collar (= on opposite side of the rounded edges of fans). Continue downwards along the outer edges of the fans as follows: *ch 5, 1 sc in the 2nd dc of the 3 dc of first group; rep from* up to and including the last group; end with ch 5 and join into a ring above the first dc along the top edge. Make a suitably large ch loop (big enough for the button) and secure with 1 sl st into the same dc. Cut yarn and fasten off. Sew on button.

Collar B

With Color 2, ch 126. Beginning in 2nd ch from hook, work 125 sc. Turn and work one more row in sc, *at the same time* increasing 11 sts evenly spaced across = 136 sc. Change to Color 1 and work in pattern:

Row 1: Ch 4, 1 dc in 1st ch, *skip 3 sc, 6 dc in next dc, skip 3 sc, (1 dc, ch 1, 1 dc) in next sc; rep from * across.

Row 2: Ch 3 (= 1st dc), 3 dc in ch-1 loop, *(1 dc, ch 1, 1 dc) between 3rd and 4th of next dc group, 6 dc in next ch loop; rep from * across, ending with 4 dc in last ch loop.

Row 3: Ch 5 (= 1 dc + ch 2), 1 dc between 1st and 2nd dc of previous row,*6 dc in ch loop, (1 dc, ch 2, 1 dc) between 3rd and 4th dc of next dc group; rep from * across.

Row 4: Ch 3 (= 1st dc), 3 dc in ch loop, *(1 dc, ch 2, 1 dc) between 3rd and 4th dc of next dc group, 8 dc in next ch loop; rep from * across, ending with 4 dc in last ch loop.

Row 5: Ch 5 (= 1 dc + ch 2), 1 dc between 1st and 2nd dc of previous row,*8 dc in ch loop, (1 dc, ch 2, 1 dc) between 4th and 5th dc of next dc group; rep from * across, ending with 1 dc between 3rd and 4th dc of last dc group.

Row 6: Work as for Row 4; cut yarn and fasten off.

Change to Color 2. Begin at top of left side and work in sc down short edge. Work 3 sc at lower corner before you continue along lower edge (= 137) sc. Work 3 sc in opposite corner and continue up the other short edge with the same number of sts as on left side. Work in sc along the neck edge. Now make a picot edging (see page 141) along short ends and outermost edge. Finish with sc along the neck edge. Cut yarn and fasten off.

Make two chains each about 9¾ in / 25 cm long with Color 2 and ch st. Sew a chain securely at top on each side. Weave in all ends neatly on WS.

Gold Clutch Bag

YOU DON'T NEED TO HAVE MUCH CROCHET EXPERIENCE TO MAKE
YOUR OWN CLUTCH BAG IF YOU JUST FOLLOW THE INSTRUCTIONS.

Yarn: Gullfasan from Dale Garn (CYCA #3 [DK/light worsted], 90% rayon/10% nylon, 136 yd/124 m / 50 g), 100 g gold

Notions: A bag frame about 8¾ in / 22 cm wide (use one from an old bag if possible, but you can also buy frames at craft stores, 9¾ x 11¾ in / 25 x 30 cm fabric for lining

Crochet Hook: U.S. size C-2 or D-3 / 2.5 or 3 mm

Gauge: 6 groups at lower edge = 4 in / 10 cm. Adjust hook size to obtain correct gauge if necessary.

Measurements: The bag is worked in one piece measuring approx. 9½ in / 24 cm wide and 11¾ in / 30 cm long

Pattern: multiple of 4 sts.

Row 1: Ch the specified number of sts. Work 4 dc in the 4th ch from hook, skip 4 ch, 1 sc in next st, *ch 3, 4 dc in 1 st (= 1 group), skip 3 ch, 1 sc in next ch; rep from * across.

Row 2: Turn with ch 3, 4 dc in 1st sc, *1 sc in ch loop of next group, ch 3, 4 dc in same ch loop; rep from * and end with 1 sc ch loop of last group.
Repeat Row 2.

FRONT AND BACK
Ch 56. Work in pattern (= 13 groups). After 15 rows, the first half is complete. For the second half, work 15 rows in pattern, beginning on opposite side of foundation chain. On the first row, insert the hook into the same stitches as previously.
Cut yarn and fasten off.

Finishing
Fold the bag at the foundation chain. Cut out the lining fabric with a ⅜ in / 1 cm seam allowance at the sides and top. Position lining in bag and sew in by hand. Sew the frame to the bag.

Tunisian Crochet Clutch Bag

IT'S FUN TO MAKE YOUR OWN BAG. THIS ONE WILL NEVER GO OUT OF FASHION!

Yarn: Gullfasan from Dale Garn (CYCA #3 [DK/light worsted], 90% rayon/10% nylon, 136 yd/124 m / 50 g), 100 g silver

Notions: A bag frame about 8¾ in / 22 cm wide (use one from an old bag if possible, but you can also buy frames at craft stores, 9½ x 15¾ in / 24 x 40 cm fabric for lining

Crochet Hook: U.S. size D-3 / 3 mm

Gauge: 24 sts and 22 rows = 4 x 4 in / 10 x 10 cm. Adjust hook size to obtain correct gauge if necessary.

Measurements: One side of the bag measures approx. 8¾ in / 22 cm wide and 7 in / 18 cm long

Pattern: See page 156, "Tunisian crochet."

FRONT AND BACK

Ch 60 and work back and forth as described for Tunisian crochet (= 59 sts across) until piece measures 14¼ in / 36 cm long = 82 rows. End with 1 row sc; cut thread and fasten off.

Finishing

Fold bag in half with RS facing out. Beginning at lower edge at the fold, join with sc up to frame (see photo); turn and work back as follows: *ch 3 (= ch loop), skip next sc, work 1 sc in next st; rep from* all the way down (the stitch count doesn't matter but should be evenly spaced) and end 1 sc before the fold. Turn and work 3 sc in each ch loop all the way up. Repeat on the opposite side. Cut out lining with a ⅜ in / 1 cm seam allowance at the sides and top. Position lining in bag and sew in by hand. Sew the frame to the bag by hand, working through both layers.

Mittens and Hat with Easy Stitches

I GOT THE PATTERN FOR THESE MITTENS FROM A CUSTOMER AT OUR YARN STORE. SHE VERY KINDLY HELPED ME BY "SCRIBBLING" DOWN THE INSTRUCTIONS ON A PIECE OF PAPER. THE HAT IS WORKED THE SAME WAY.

Mittens

The mittens are worked in a way that makes them an easy project for beginners. The methods for increasing and decreasing are a little different but very simple. The stitches swirl around so it is important to mark the beginning of the round. I have crocheted the design and recommend that you not work too loosely. The stitches are all single crochet worked through back loops only so there will be horizontal "stripes" throughout. Best of all, both mittens are alike and there is no difference between the left and right mittens. Try it!

Sizes: S (M)
Yarn: Eskimo from Drops (CYCA #6 [bulky/roving], 100% wool, 54 y/49 m / 50 g), 100 g Light Pine Green
Crochet hook: U.S. size J-10 / 6 mm
Gauge: 13 sc = 4 in / 10 cm. Adjust hook size to obtain correct gauge if necessary.

Increases: Increase 1 st by working ch 1 between 2 sts. On the next rnd, sc into ch loop.
Decreases: Decrease by skipping 1 st.

Ch 6 and join into a ring with 1 sl st into 1st ch.

Rnd 1: Ch 1, (1 sc, ch 1) 6 times around ring = 12 sc.

Rnd 2: From this rnd on, always work sc through back loops only (see page 155 in the Crochet School section). Mark 1st st of rnd and move marker up on every rnd. (1 sc in each of next 3 sts, ch 1) around = 4 sts increased; 16 sts total.

Rnd 3: Sc around (= 1 sc in each sc and in each ch) = 16 sc.

Rnd 4: (Sc 1 in each of next 4 sts, ch 1) around = 20 sts. All increases for size S complete.

Rnds 5–14: For size M, increase 2 sts evenly spaced on Rnd 6 and then continue without further shaping. At this point, check the length to make sure it reaches the thumbhole.

Rnd 15: For size M, work 1 rnd in sc. For size S, make the thumbhole (the same way for left and right mittens) as follows: ch 6, skip 6 sts, continue around in sc and end with 6 sc into chain for thumbhole = 20 sts.

Rnd 16: For size S. work 1 rnd in sc.
For size M: make the thumbhole (the same way for left and right mittens) as follows: ch 7, skip

»——→

7 sts, continue around in sc and end with 7 sc into chain for thumbhole = 22 sts.

Rnds 17–19: Work around in sc = 20 (22) sc.

Rnd 20: Size S: decrease 2 sts evenly spaced around. Size M: sc around.

Rnd 21: Size S: sc around. Size M: decrease 2 sts evenly spaced around.

Rnd 22: Size S: increase 2 sts evenly spaced around. Size M: sc around.

Rnds 23–27: Size S: sc around. Size M: increase 2 sts evenly spaced on Rnd 23 and then sc around through Rnd 27 or until mitten is desired length. Cut yarn and draw end through last st.

THUMB

Work 14–16 sc around thumbhole. On 2nd rnd, decrease 2 sts evenly spaced around. Continue with 12–14 sc around for 4-5 rnds. On each of the next 2 rnds, skip every other st. Cut yarn and draw end through rem sts.

Make the second mitten the same way. Sew any holes at thumbhole closed and weave in all ends on WS.

Hat

This hat is as simply worked as the mittens. The stitches spiral around, so it is important that you mark the 1st st of the rnd and move up marker every rnd.

Sizes: S (M, L)
Yarn: Eskimo from Drops (CYCA #6 [bulky/roving], 100% wool, 54 y/49 m / 50 g), 100 (150, 150) g Light Pine Green
Crochet hook: U.S. size J-10 / 6 mm
Gauge: 13 sc = 4 in / 10 cm. Adjust hook size to obtain correct gauge if necessary.

Increases: Increase 1 st by working ch 1 between 2 sts. On the next rnd, sc into ch loop.
Decreases: Decrease by skipping 1 st.
Begin each rnd with ch 1 instead of 1st ch.

Ch 6 and join into a ring with 1 sl st into 1st ch.

Rnd 1: (1 sc, ch 1) 6 times around ring = 12 sc.

Rnd 2: From this rnd on, always work sc through back loops only (see page 155 in the Crochet School section). Work as for Rnd 1 = 24 sc.

Rnd 3: Sc around = 24 sc.

Rnd 4: Work (2 sc, ch 1) around = 36 sc.

Rnd 5: Sc around.

Rnd 6: Increase 6 sts evenly spaced around = 42 st.

Rnd 7: Increase 8 sts evenly spaced around = 50 sc; this is the last increase rnd for size S.

Rnd 8: Increase 6 sts evenly spaced around = 56 sc; this is the last increase rnd for size M.

Rnd 9: Increase 10 sts evenly spaced around = 66 sc; this is the last increase rnd for size L. Continue around in sc until hat measures approx. 10¼ in / 26 cm or desired length. Cut yarn and weave in all ends neatly on WS.

*Mittens and hat
with easy stitches*

Headband

THIS IS A MODERN VERSION OF A HEADBAND STYLE POPULAR IN THE 1950S. IT IS PRACTICAL AND DECORATIVE. THE BAND IS MADE IN TWO PIECES AND CROCHETED WITH TWO STRANDS OF YARN HELD TOGETHER. STITCHES ARE WORKED THROUGH BACK LOOPS ONLY.

Size: Women's
Measurements: 20–20½ in / 51–52 cm. The band is elastic and will stretch to fit most heads.
Yarn: Fine Alpaca (Tynn Alpakka) from Du Store Alpakka (CYCA #1 [sock/fingering/baby], 100% alpaca, 183 yd/167 m / 50 g), 50 g of Color 1: Sand Heather
+ Baby Silk from Du Store Alpakka (CYCA #2 [sport/baby], 80% baby alpaca/20% silk/, 145 yd/133 m / 50 g), 50 g of Color 2: Natural
Crochet Hook: U.S. size J-10 / 6 mm
Gauge: 13 sc = 4 in / 10 cm. Adjust hook size to obtain correct gauge if necessary.

Holding one strand of each yarn together, loosely ch enough sts to go around your head. Try on the chain to make sure it fits. For the headband shown here, we begin with 62 ch. Join chain into a ring with 1 sl st into 1st ch. Work in dc around through back loops only until band measures 4¼ in / 12 cm or desired height. Cut yarn and weave in ends on WS.

SMALL BAND TO GATHER IN CENTER FRONT

Begin with a ch about 6 in / 15 cm long. Work back and forth in dc, alternating rows with sts in front and back loops (see page 155 in the Crochet School section). Continue until piece measures 2 in / 5 cm.

Finishing
Place the small band around the headband and pull it in so that it gathers the headband in somewhat. Sew down. Cut yarn and weave in end on WS.

Bobble Hat

YOU CAN CROCHET THIS HAT AS EASY AS 1−2−3! IT IS WORKED FROM
THE BRIM UP. THE TECHNIQUE WE USED WAS OFTEN USED FOR BABY
BLANKETS PREVIOUSLY AND PRODUCES A SOFT AND FLUFFY ITEM.
THE MOTIF CAN ALSO BE USED FOR HATS FOR CHILDREN AND ADULTS,
MAYBE WITH A STRAP UNDER THE CHIN FOR CHILDREN.

Here's a new and colorful version of a hat! Of course, you can make it in one color only if you want!

Sizes: S/M (M/L), depending on number of stitches and hook size.
Yarn: Hubro from Dale Garn (CYCA #6 [bulky/roving], 100% wool, 72 yd/66 m / 100 g
Yarn Amounts: 100 g of each color
Color Combination A: Color 1: Cerise, Color 2: Yellow, Color 3: Red, Color 4: Orange
Color Combination B: Color 1: Petroleum, Color 2: Lime, Color 3: Blue, Color 4: Green
Crochet Hook: U.S. size K-10½ / 7 mm for S/M or U.S. size L-11 / 8 mm for M/L

Pattern:
Bobbles: Yoh, insert hook through the st below and bring yarn through, stretching loop to about ¾ in / 2 cm. (Yoh, bring a new loop through the same st and stretch it) 2 times = a total of 3 yarnovers + 3 loops = 7 loops on hook. Yoh and through all the loops on the hook, and end with ch 1 = 1 bobble. Make sure that you do not work too tightly.
NOTE: The last bobble of the round should be finished by drawing the yarnover through all 7 loops on the hook, ch 1, change to color for next rnd and join last bobble to the 1st bobble on the rnd with 1 sl st in top of bobble.

By working around this way, you will see that the rounds automatically shift slightly to the left. Make sure you work following the instructions below. The 1st bobble on each rnd begins by stretching the yarn loop already on the hook before the yoh, etc. The remaining bobbles begin with 1 yarnover, bring yarn through, etc.

With Color 1, loosely ch 48 and join into a ring with 1 sl st into 1st ch.

Rnd 1: Begin rnd by stretching the loop on the hook to about ¾ in / 2 cm long; work bobble in the 1st ch. Work a bobble into every other st = 24 bobbles. Secure last bobble to the first on the rnd with 1 sl st into top of bobble, using Color 2.

Rnd 2: Begin the first bobble in the space between bobbles 1 and 2 of previous rnd. Continue around with 1 bobble between bobbles = 24 bobbles. End with Color 2 and 1 sl st.

Rnd 3: Begin the 1st bobble in the space between the 1st and last bobbles of previous rnd so the color shifts will stack one over the other. Continue around with 1 bobble between 2 bobbles of previous rnd = 24 bobbles. End with 1 sl st using Color 4.

Rnd 4: With Color 4, work as for Rnd 2.

Rnd 5: With Color 1, work as for Rnd 3.

Rnd 6: With Color 2, work as for Rnd 2.

Rnd 7: With Color 3, work as for Rnd 3. Change to Color 4.

Rnd 8: Decrease by 3 bobbles on this round as follows: **Work 6 bobbles, join the next 2 bobbles: *with 2 instead of 3 yoh in the first space, leave loops on hook; rep from * in next space. Yoh and through all 9 loops *at the same time*, ch 1; rep from ** two more times. End rnd as set, changing colors.

Decrease bobbles on the next rnd the same way, with 1 less bobble between each joined bobble—work 5 bobbles and then join 2 bobbles. On the next rnd, work 4 bobbles and then join 2 bobbles, etc. Continue the same way until there are only 3 bobbles left.

Cut yarn, leaving a long tail and pull end through last st. Thread end into tapestry needle and use it to close opening at top.

Make a pompom with Color 1 and sew it securely to top of hat (see page 165 in the Crochet School section).

Weave in ends neatly on WS.

Bobble hat

Sporty Hat

HERE'S A NICE AND COMFY HAT FOR GIRLS AND BOYS, WOMEN AND MEN. IT WILL LOOK JUST AS GOOD FOR SCHOOL AS ON THE SKI TRAIL. IT'S CROCHETED FROM THE TOP DOWN AND CAN BE MULTI- OR SINGLE-COLOR.

Sizes: 1 (4, 8 years, women's, men's)
Finished Measurements:
Head circumference: 17¼ (19¾, 22, 22¾, 23¾) in / 44 (50, 56, 58, 60) cm
Length: approx. 8¾ (9, 9½, 10¼, 10¾) in / 22 (23, 24, 26, 27) cm

Yarn: Freestyle from Dale Garn (CYCA #4 [worsted/afghan/aran], 100% wool, 88 yd/80 m / 50 g)
Yarn Amounts: 50 g each of:
Blue hat: Color 1: Mint, Color 2: Sea Blue, Color 3: Ice Blue, Color 4: Dark Gray
Pink hat: Color 1: Mint, Color 2: Bright Pink, Color 3: Pink, Color 4: Dark Gray
Crochet Hook: U.S. size H-8 / 5 mm
Gauge: 14 dc or 7 sc/dc groups = 4 in / 10 cm. Adjust hook size to obtain correct gauge if necessary.

Abbreviations and Stitches

sc/dc gr: joined sc and dc group: *1 sc (bring yarn only through 1 loop on hook), + 1 dc (when bringing through for last step of dc, bring yarn through all 3 loops on hook *at the same time*), yoh, bring yarn through loop on hook once more.
NOTE: there are only 2 sts on the 1ˢᵗ sc/dc group of the rnd.

Increases: Increase with 8 new sc/dc gr on each increase rnd = 16, 24, 32 sc/dc gr, etc.
Decreases (joining 2 sc/dc gr): Work 1 sc/dc gr but do not bring yarn through the last 3 loops on hook; make a sc/dc gr in next space but do not bring yarn through the last 2 loops on hook, yoh and through all 5 loops on hook at the same time.
Color Changes: Work 2 rnds with each color

in sequence from Color 1 through Color 4 and repeat. Begin color changes on Rnd 3.

NOTE: Beginning on Rnd 2, make ch 1 instead of 1ˢᵗ sc.

Blue Hat

Sizes: 1 (4, 8 years, women's, men's)

With Color 1, ch 6 and join into a ring with 1 sl st into 1ˢᵗ ch.

Rnd 1 (Color 1): Begin with ch 3 (= 1ˢᵗ dc), work 15 dc around ring = 16 dc total; end with 1 sl st into top of ch 3.

Rnd 2 (Color 1): Work 1 sc/dc gr into sl st, and then 1 sc/dc gr in each dc around; end with 1 sl st into top of 1ˢᵗ sc/dc gr.

Rnd 3 (Color 2): Beginning in space of previous rnd, work 1 sc/dc gr between every sc/dc gr of previous rnd; end with 1 sl st into top of 1ˢᵗ sc/dc gr.

Rnd 4: Beginning in space of previous rnd, alternately work 1 sc/dc gr in one space and 2 sc/dc gr in next space = 24 sc/dc gr; end with 1 sl st into top of 1ˢᵗ sc/dc gr.

Rnd 5 (Color 3): Work as for Rnd 3.

Rnd 6: Beginning in space of previous rnd, work (1 sc/dc gr in each of next two spaces and 2 sc/dc gr in next space) around = 32 sc/dc gr; end with 1 sl st into top of 1ˢᵗ sc/dc gr. This is the last increase rnd for size 1 year.
For all larger sizes [4, 8 years, women's, men's], increase on Rnd 7: 2 (4, 6, 8) more sc/dc gr evenly spaced around = 34 (36, 38, 40) sc/dc gr total.

Repeat Rnd 3 until 1¼ in / 3 cm before finished length.

With Color 2, work 2 rnds with 64 (68, 72, 76, 80) dc around = 1 dc in each sc/dc gr and each space in between groups; end with 1 sl st into top of 1ˢᵗ st.

If the hat is too wide, decrease 6 (6, 6, 8, 8) sts evenly spaced on last rnd. Work more rnds if desired.

Cut yarn and weave in all ends neatly on WS.

Tip

To avoid weaving in all the ends afterwards, catch the ends as you work. See page 152 in the Crochet School section.

Using all 4 colors, make a pompom and sew securely to the top of hat. See page 165 in the Crochet School section.

Pink Hat

Sizes: 1 (4, 8 years, women's)

Work as for Blue Hat, but continue increasing (after Rnd 6) on every other rnd with 1 sc/dc gr more between each increase through Rnd 12 = 56 sc/dc gr. Stop increasing for all sizes at this point. For women's size, work 3 rnds with 1 sc/dc gr between each group. Continue, beginning with Rnd 13:

Rnd 13: Work as for Rnd 3 of Blue Hat.

Rnd 14: Begin decreasing as follows: Work (5 sc/dc gr, work a joined group) around = 48 groups rem.

Rnd 15: Work as for Rnd 3 of Blue Hat.

Rnd 16: For all sizes, decrease: Work (4 sc/dc gr, work a joined group) around = 40 groups rem.

Rnd 17: Work as for Rnd 3 of Blue Hat.

Rnd 18: Decrease 8 (6, 4, 2) sc/dc gr evenly spaced around = 32 (34, 36, 38) groups rem.

Crochet to finished (or desired) length as for Blue Hat.

End with 2 rnds: work 64 (68, 72, 76) dc evenly spaced around = 1 dc in each sc/dc gr and each space; end with 1 sl st into top of 1ˢᵗ dc.

If the hat is too wide, decrease 6 (6, 6, 8) sts evenly spaced on last rnd. Work more rnds if desired.

LACE EDGING (multiple of 6 sts)

Adjust stitch count as necessary for a multiple of 6.

All sizes: 1 sc in 1ˢᵗ dc, *skip 2 dc, work 5 dc in next dc, skip 2 dc, 1 sc in next dc) around; end with 1 sl st into 1ˢᵗ sc. Cut yarn and weave in all ends neatly on WS.

Olympic Hat

HERE'S A VARIATION ON THE POPULAR OLYMPIC HAT. IT'S THE
SAME HAT AS THE ONE WITH EASY STITCHES ON PAGE 114 BUT
THE WRONG SIDE FACES OUT ON THIS VERSION.

Sizes: S (M, L)
Yarn: Eskimo from Drops (CYCA #6
[bulky/roving], 100% wool, 54 y/49 m / 50
g), 100 (150, 150) g Light Blue and 50 (50,
50) g Red
Crochet Hook: U.S. size J-10 / 6 mm
Gauge: 13 sc = 4 in / 10 cm. Adjust hook
size to obtain correct gauge if necessary.

Work as for Hat with Easy Stitches. Turn
hat inside out and then work 3 rnds sc with
Red. Cut yarn and fasten off.

Olympic hat

Chevron-Striped Cowl

A PRETTY COWL WITH DECORATIVE CHEVRON STRIPES.

Yarn: Fine Alpaca (Tynn Alpakka) from Du Store Alpakka (CYCA #1 [sock/fingering/baby], 100% alpaca, 183 yd/167 m / 50 g), 50 g each of **Color 1**: Rose and **Color 2**: Pink
Iris Alpaca from Rauma (CYCA #5 [chunky/craft/rug], 74% alpaca, 22% wool, 4% nylon, 142 yd/130 m / 50 g), 50 g of **Color 3**: Red
Alpaca from SandnesGarn, (CYCA #3 [DK/light worsted], 100% alpaca, 120 yd/110 m / 50 g), 50 g each of **Color 4**: Burgundy, **Color 5**: Cerise, and **Color 6**: Red

Crochet Hook: U.S. size J-10 / 6 mm
Finished Measurements: Circumference approx. 59 in / 150 cm

Stripe Sequence:
All of the stripes (except for Color 2) are worked with 2 strands held together.
2 rnds Color 1
3 rnds Color 3
1 rnd Color 2
3 rnds Color 5
1 rnd Color 1
2 rnds Color 4
2 rnds Color 6
3 rnds Color 5
1 rnd Color 1
3 rnds Color 3
= a total of 21 rnds.

With two strands of Color 1 held together, loosely ch 188; join into a ring with 1 sl st into 1st ch. Continue in pattern with doubled yarn and stripe sequence as described above. Change the color when ending the rnd with 1 sl st.

Rnd 1: Ch 3, 1 dc in each of next 4 ch, *skip 2 ch, 1 dc in each of next 4 ch, (1 dc, ch 2, 1 dc) in next ch, 1 dc in each of next 4 ch; rep from * until 6 ch rem. Skip 2 ch, 1 dc in each of next 4 ch, 1 dc in same st as beg ch-3, ch 2; end with 1 sl st into top of ch 3 at beg of rnd.

Rnd 2: Ch 3, 1 dc in each of next 3 dc, *skip 2 sts, 1 dc in each of next 4 dc, (1 dc, ch 2, 1 dc) in next ch loop, 1 dc in each of next 4 dc; rep from * until 6 dc rem. Skip 2 sts, 1 dc in each of next 4 dc, (1 dc, ch 2, 1 dc) in last ch loop; end with 1 sl st into top of ch 3 at beg of rnd.

Rnd 3: Ch 3, 1 dc in same st and then each of next 2 dc, *skip 2 sts, 1 dc in each of next 4 dc, (1 dc, ch 2, 1 dc) in next ch loop, 1 dc in each of next 4 dc; rep from * until 6 dc rem. Skip 2 sts, 1 dc in each of next 4 dc, (1 dc, ch 2, 1 dc) in last ch loop; end with 1 sl st into top of ch 3 at beg of rnd.

Repeat Rnds 1–3 until all the stripes have been worked or cowl is desired length by repeating stripes.

Cut yarn and weave in all ends on WS.

The stitch count for the pattern is 12 sts + 6. Adjust the total number of stitches if desired for a larger or smaller cowl.

Chevron-striped cowl

Feminine Set

A FEMININE THREE-PIECE SET FOR THOSE COLD DAYS. EACH PIECE IS FINISHED WITH A LUXURIOUS EFFECT. CHOOSE ONE ITEM—OR WHY NOT MAKE ALL THREE? THE PATTERN IS SIMPLE TO CROCHET AND IT'S EASY TO ADJUST FOR OTHER SIZES.

Cowl

Size: Women's
Finished Measurements: approx. 8 x 55 in / 20 x 140 cm

Yarn: Kashmir Alpakka from SandnesGarn (CYCA #4 [worsted/afghan/aran], 84% alpaca, 16% cashmere, 74 yd/68 m / 50 g), 150 g Light Pink
Mini Alpaca from SandnesGarn (CYCA #1 [sock/fingering/baby], 100% alpaca, 164 yd/150 m / 50 g), 100 g Light Pink
Iris Alpaca from Rauma (CYCA #5 [chunky/craft/rug], 74% alpaca, 22% wool, 4% nylon, 142 yd/130 m / 50 g), 50 g of Light Pink
Crochet Hook: U.S. size K-10 ½ or L-11 / 7 mm
Gauge: 2 pattern groups = 4 in / 10 cm. Adjust hook size to obtain correct gauge if necessary.

The pattern is a multiple of 6 sts. If you want a wider or narrower cowl, change the total stitch count in multiples of 6.

With one strand each of Mini Alpaca and Kashmir Alpakka, ch 165.

Rnd 1: Beginning in 4th ch from hook, work 1 dc group: (1 dc, ch 1, 2 dc) in same st, skip 2 ch and continue with *(2 dc, ch 1, 2 dc) in next st, skip 2 ch, 1 dc, skip 2 ch*; rep from * across. Join into a ring with 1 sl st into 3rd ch at beg of row.

Rnd 2: Ch 3 (= 1st dc), 1 dc in center of dc group, ch 1, 2 dc in center of same dc groups, *1 dc in dc, (2 dc, ch 1, 2 dc) in center of next dc group); rep from * around and end with 1 dc in dc, 1 sl st into top of ch 3.

Rnds 3–12: Work as for Rnd 2, but insert hook into opposite side of single dc or the pattern will skew. Alternate side of single dc on every other rnd.
NOTE: On Rnds 5–6 and 11–12, substitute Iris for Kashmir Alpakka for a softer effect.
  Cut yarn and weave in all ends on WS.

Hat

The pattern makes a wavy effect along the edge near the face.

Size: Women's
Finished Measurements: approx. 8 in / 20 cm long and 22 in / 56 cm circumference

Yarn: Kashmir Alpakka from SandnesGarn (CYCA #4 [worsted/afghan/aran], 84% alpaca, 16% cashmere, 74 yd/68 m / 50 g), 100 g Light Pink
Mini Alpaca from SandnesGarn (CYCA #1 [sock/fingering/baby], 100% alpaca, 164 yd/150 m / 50 g), 50 g Light Pink
Iris Alpaca from Rauma (CYCA #5 [chunky/craft/rug], 74% alpaca, 22% wool, 4% nylon, 142 yd/130 m / 50 g), 50 g of Light Pink

Crochet Hook: U.S. size K-10 ½ or L-11 / 7 mm

Gauge: 2 pattern groups = 4 in / 10 cm. Adjust hook size to obtain correct gauge if necessary.

Pattern: See Cowl

With 1 strand each Mini Alpaca and Kashmir Alpakka held together, ch 4; join into a ring with 1 sl st into 1st ch.

Rnd 1: Ch 2 (= 1st sc), work 11 sc around ring = 12 sc total, and end with 1 sl st into 1st ch.

Rnd 2: Ch 3 (= 1st dc), 1 dc in same st, ch 1, 2 dc in same st, skip 1 sc,*(2 dc, ch 1, 2 dc) in same sc, skip 1 sc; rep from * around. End with 1 sl st into top of ch 3 = 6 dc groups.

Rnd 3: 1 sl st into ch after the first 2 dc, ch 3, 1 dc, ch 1, 2 dc in same st, *(2 dc, ch 1, 2 dc) in next space; rep from * around = 12 dc groups. End with 1 sl st into top of ch 3.

Rnd 4: 1 sl st into ch between the first 2 dc, ch 3, 1 dc, ch 1, 2 dc in same st, 1 dc before next dc group, *(2 dc, ch 1, 2 dc) in next space, 1 dc before next dc group; rep from * around. End with 1 sl st into top of ch 3.

Rnds 5–13: Work around with a single dc between each dc group. Don't forget to work on alternate sides of the single dc as described in the scarf pattern.

Try on the hat before it is completely finished. If it is too wide, change to a smaller size hook.

Change to Iris Alpaca and work 3 rnds to finished (or desired) length.

Cut yarn and weave in all end neatly on WS.

Wrist Warmers

These wrist warmers are not just decorative; they are also very warm. They make lovely gifts, especially if you take the time to sew on a few beads along the lower edge.

Size: Women's

Finished Measurements: approx. 9¾ x 4¾ in / 25 x 12 cm

Yarn: Kashmir Alpakka from Sandnes (CYCA #4 [worsted/afghan/aran], 84% alpaca, 16% cashmere, 74 yd/68 m / 50 g), 50 g Light Pink Mini Alpaca from SandnesGarn (CYCA #1 [sock/fingering/baby], 100% alpaca, 164 yd/150 m / 50 g), 50 g Light Pink Iris Alpaca from Rauma (CYCA #5 [chunky/craft/rug], 74% alpaca, 22% wool, 4% nylon, 142 yd/130 m / 50 g), 50 g of Light Pink

Crochet Hook: U.S. size K-10 ½ or L-11 / 7 mm and U.S. size H-8 / 5 mm

Gauge: 2 pattern groups with larger size hook = 4 in / 10 cm. Adjust hook size to obtain correct gauge if necessary.

Pattern: See Cowl

Begin at the top and work down towards the wrist. With larger size hook and 1 strand each Mini Alpaca and Kashmir Alpakka held together, loosely ch 30. Join into a ring with 1 sl st into 1st ch. Work as for scarf (= 5 repeats).

After 10 rnds, change to smaller size hook. If the wrist warmer seems a bit too wide, change to smaller hook 2 or 3 rnds sooner.

After completing 12 rnds, make the lower edge and thumbhole. Substitute Iris Alpaca for the Kashmir Alpakka. Work to the last repeat of the round. Ch 5 after the 4th dc in a dc group. Skip the single dc and work the next dc group. Continue around. On the next rnd, work 1 sl st into thte 3rd of the 5 ch for the thumbhole before continuing with dc groups. If desired, work another 2 rounds as previously. Cut yarn and weave in all ends on WS.

Make another wrist warmer the same way, but with the thumbhole on the opposite side.

Feminine set

Double Crochet Hats

THE PATTERN IS THE SAME BUT THE YARN MAKES ALL THE DIFFERENCE. THE BRIM IS WORKED LAST. CHANGE TO A SMALLER/LARGER HOOK IF THE HAT IS TOO LARGE/SMALL.

Size: One size
Yarn:
Brown Hat: Nepal from Drops (CYCA #4 [worsted/afghan/aran], 65% wool, 35% alpaca, 82 yd/75 m / 50 g), 100 g Camel)
Alpaca from Drops (CYCA #2 [sport/baby], 100% alpaca, 182 yd/166 m / 50 g), 50 g Light Beige
Concorde from Rauma CYCA #0 [lace/fingering], 64% rayon, 36% polyester, 273 yd/250 m / 25 g), 50 g Gold
The hat is worked with 1 strand of each yarn held together.
White Hat: Iris Alpaca from Rauma (CYCA #5 [chunky/craft/rug], 74% alpaca, 22% wool, 4% nylon, 142 yd/130 m / 50 g), 50 g of White
1 spool of Bling sequin thread from Du Store Alpakka (CYCA #0 [lace/fingering], 100% polyester, 382 yd/349 m / 50 g), 50 g Silver
The hat is worked with 1 strand each of Iris Alpaca and Bling for top of hat; add Concorde for brim.
Concorde from Rauma (CYCA #0 [lace/fingering], 64% rayon, 36% polyester, 273 yd/250 m / 25 g), 50 g Silver

Crochet Hook: U.S. sizes L-11 and J-10 / 8 and 6 mm.
Gauge: 8-9 sc with larger size hook = 4 in / 10 cm

With one strand of each yarn held together (as indicated above) and larger size hook, ch 4 and join into a ring with 1 sl st into 1st ch.

Rnd 1: Ch 2 (= 1st sc), work 5 sc around ring = 6 sc total; join with 1 sl st into 2nd ch.

Rnd 2: Ch 3 (= 1st sc + ch 1), (1 sc in next sc, ch 1) around and end with 1 sl st into 2nd ch = 12 sc.

Rnd 3: Ch 3, (1 dc in next st, 2 dc in next st) around and end with 1 sl st into top of ch 3 = 18 dc.

Rnds 4-7: Work as for Rnd 3, but with 1 dc more between increases = 42 dc.

Rnds 8-14: Work 1 dc over each dc around.

Rnds 15-19: Change to smaller size hook and work around in sc for the brim.
Cut yarn and weave in ends neatly on WS.

Double crochet hats

Three Hats— One Pattern

THESE THREE HATS ARE ALL WORKED FROM THE SAME PATTERN.

Size: Women's

Yarn:

Gray Hat: Puno Alpaca from Rauma (CYCA #5 [chunky/craft/rug], 68% baby alpaca, 10% extra fine Merino wool, 22% polyamide, 120 yd/110 m / 50 g), 100 g Gray Metallic; Bling sequin yarn from Du Store Alpakka (CYCA #0 [lace/fingering], 100% polyester, 382 yd/349 m / 50 g), 1 spool Gray about 10 m thin reflective yarn

Flower: 1 strand each of Puno and Bling held together

Pink Hat: Iris Alpaca from Rauma (CYCA #5 [chunky/craft/rug], 74% alpaca, 22% wool, 4% nylon, 142 yd/130 m / 50 g), 100 g Light Pink Mini Alpaca from SandnesGarn CYCA #1 [sock/fingering/baby], 100% alpaca, 164 yd/150 m / 50 g), 50 g Light Pink Bling sequin yarn from Du Store Alpakka (CYCA #0 [lace/fingering], 100% polyester, 382 yd/349 m / 50 g), 1 spool Silver Gray or White

Hold 1 strand each of Iris Alpaca, Mini Alpaca, and Bling together for hat.

Flower: 1 strand each of Iris Alpaca and Mini Alpaca held together

Light Blue Hat: Iris Alpaca from Rauma (CYCA #5 [chunky/craft/rug], 74% alpaca, 22% wool, 4% nylon, 142 yd/130 m / 50 g), 100 g Light Blue

Fine Alpaca (Tynn Alpakka) from Du Store Alpakka (CYCA #1 [sock/fingering/baby], 100% alpaca, 183 yd/167 m / 50 g), 100 g Light Blue

London from SandnesGarn (CYCA #0 [lace/fingering], 100% synthetic effect yarn, 164 yd/150 m / 50 g), 50 g Silver

Bling sequin yarn from Du Store Alpakka (CYCA #0 [lace/fingering], 100% polyester, 382 yd/349 m / 50 g), 1 spool White or Light Gray

Top of Hat: Hold 1 strand each Iris Alpaca and Fine Alpaca together

Brim: Hold 1 strand each Fine Alpaca and London together.

Three hats— one pattern

Flower: Hold 1 strand each Iris Alpaca, Fine Alpaca, London, and sequin yarn together.

Crochet Hook: U.S. sizes J-10 and G-6 / 6 and 4 mm.

Gauge:

Light Blue and Pink Hats: approx. 10 sc with larger size hook = 4 in / 10 cm

Gray Hat: approx. 11 sc with larger hook = 4 in / 10 cm.

Adjust hook size to obtain correct gauge if necessary.

NOTE: Before starting any of the hats, see yarn details above.

With larger size hook, ch 4 and join into a ring with 1 sl st into 1st ch.

Rnd 1: Ch 2 (= 1st sc), work 11 sc around ring = 12 sc total. End with 1 sl st into 2nd ch.

Rnd 2: Ch 2, (1 sc into next st, 2 sc into next st) around and end with 1 sl st into 2nd ch = 18 sc total.

Rnds 3–7: Work as for Rnd 2 but with 1 more sc between increases on each rnd.

Rnd 8: Sc around.

Rnd 9: Try on hat. If necessary, work 6 increases evenly spaced around.

Rnd 10 onward: Work around in sc until hat is desired length before brim. The longer it is, the baggier. If necessary, decrease 4-6 sts on the last round.

BRIM

With smaller hook, work 4-5 rounds in sc. Finish the Pink and Light Blue hats with a picot edging (see page 141). Cut yarn and weave in ends neatly on WS.

FLOWER

With larger hook and 1 strand each of the yarns specified above held together, ch 5 and join into a ring with 1 sl st into 1st ch.

Rnd 1: Ch 1 and work 13 sc around ring = 14 sc.

End with 1 sl st into 1st ch.

Rnd 2: (1 sc, ch 3, skip 1 st) 7 times = 7 ch loops. End with 1 sl st into 1st sc.

Rnd 3: 1 sl st into ch loop. In each of the ch-3 loops, work (1 sc, 3 dc, 1 sc).

Rnd 4: (1 sc behind petal in sc of 2nd rnd, ch 5) 7 times. End with 1 sl st into ch loop.

Rnd 5: In each of the 7 ch loops around, work (1 sc, 5 dc, 1 sc).

Rnd 6: (1 sc behind petal in sc of 4th rnd, ch 7) 7 times. End with 1 sl st into 1st sc.

Rnd 7: In each of the 7 ch loops around, work (1 sc, 7 dc, 1 sc).

Rnd 8: If desired, work a round of sc using reflective yarn.

Sew flower securely to hat.

Three hats—
one pattern

Lace Scarf

A PRETTY LACE SCARF THAT YOU CAN MAKE AS LONG AS YOU LIKE. IF YOU WANT A WIDER SCARF, ADD STITCHES IN A MULTIPLE OF 5. THE ENTIRE SCARF IS CROCHETED WITH TWO STRANDS OF YARN HELD TOGETHER. [Design: Daledesign]

Measurements: 7½ in / 19 cm wide x 82½ in / 210 cm long

Yarn: Alpaca from Dale Garn (CYCA #2 [sport/ baby], 100% alpaca, 145 yd/133 m / 50 g), 300 g of Color 1: Mint and 50 g Color 2: Light Gray

Crochet Hook: U.S. size L-11 / 8 mm

With 2 strands of Color 1 held together, ch 31.

Row 1: Beginning in 2nd ch from hook, sc across = 30 sc.

Row 2: Ch 3, work 1 dc in 1st sc, skip 3 sc, *(2 dc, ch 1, 2 dc) in next sc (= ch loop), skip 4 sts and repeat from * across. end with skip 3 sc, 2 dc in last sc.

Row 3: Ch 3, 1 dc in 1st dc, *(2 dc, ch 1, 2 dc) in next ch loop. Repeat from * across, ending with 2 dc in last dc.

Repeat Row 3 until scarf is about 78¾ in / 200 cm long or desired length.

LACE EDGING FOR BOTH ENDS OF THE SCARF

With two strands of Color 2 held together, attach yarn with 1 sl st to one end. Ch 3, 2 tr in sl st, *1 sc between dc groups, 5 tr in ch loop; rep from * across, ending with 3 tr and 1 sl st into last st.

Cut yarn and weave in all ends neatly on WS.

Slippers with Bows

A PAIR OF THICK, WARM SLIPPERS IN NO TIME AT ALL!

Yarn: Hubro from Dale Garn (CYCA #6 [bulky/roving], 100% wool, 72 yd/66 m / 100 g), 200 g Light Blue
Alpaca from Dale Garn (CYCA #2 [sport/baby], 100% alpaca, 145 yd/133 m / 50 g), 50 g Beige
Crochet Hook: U.S. size J-10 / 6 mm, U.S. size H-8 / 5 mm for bows, and U.S. size D-3 / 3 mm for lace edging
Size: U.S. sizes 8-10 / European 38-41 (the slippers are stretchy)

With largest hook, ch 21.
Beginning in 2nd ch from hook, work 20 sc. Work back and forth in sc for 5½-6 in / 14-15 cm. At the end of the next row, ch 5 and begin working in the round. Continue in sc around until slipper is 8¾ in / 22 cm long (or to top of little toe).
Shape toe on the next 5 rnds:

Toe Rnd 1: (5 sc, 2 sc tog) 4 times = 21 sc rem.

Toe Rnd 2: (4 sc, 2 sc tog) 4 times = 17 sc rem.

Toe Rnd 3: (3 sc, 2 sc tog) 4 times = 13 sc rem.

Toe Rnd 4: (2 sc, 2 sc tog) 4 times = 9 sc rem.

Toe Rnd 5: 1 sc in each st around = 9 sc rem. Turn slipper inside out and seam toe. Cut yarn and fasten off.

With RS facing, alpaca yarn and smallest hook, work an even number of sc around the ankle opening. Work 1 rnd dc fans as follows: Work 7 dc in the 1st sc, *skip next sc, 1 sc in next sc, skip next sc, work 7 dc in next sc; rep from * around. Make sure that you have the same number of fans on each slipper.

BOWS (make 2 alike)

With U.S. size H-8 / 5 mm crochet hook and two strands of Alpaca yarn held together, ch 10; turn and work back and forth in sc for 1½ in / 4 cm.
Cut yarn and fasten off. Using slipper yarn, sew the bows to each slipper centered on instep.

Swatch 1
CLUSTER PATTERN

Swatch 2
STAR PATTERN

Swatch 3
SWEDISH WOVEN PATTERN

Swatch 4
CLIMBING CLUSTERS

Swatch 5
LINKED DOUBLE CROCHET
CLUSTERS

Swatch 6
NETTING PATTERN

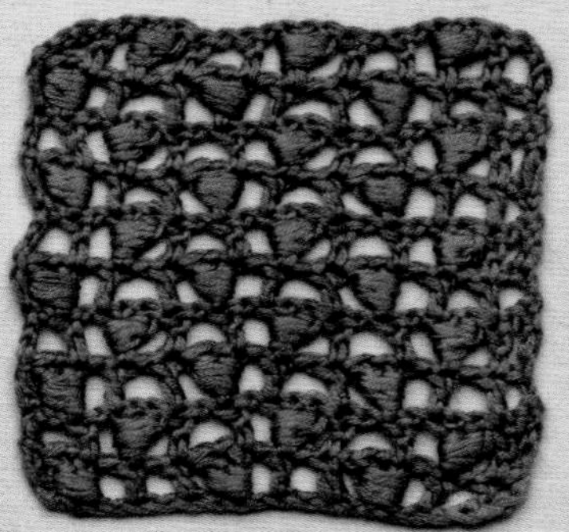

Swatch 7
SHELL PATTERN

Swatch 8
LACE PATTERN

Swatch 9
PEACOCK PATTERN

Swatches

THESE SWATCHES REPRESENT WELL-KNOWN PATTERNS THAT HAVE BEEN CROCHETED FOR GENERATIONS. TRY THE VARIOUS TECHNIQUES SO YOU WILL LEARN SOMETHING NEW AT THE SAME TIME. WE USED VARIOUS FINE COTTON YARNS.

Swatch 1
CLUSTER PATTERN

Multiple of 5 + 8 stitches

1 cluster (cl) = Yoh, insert hook into ch and bring up a loop, (yoh, bring through 1 more loop) 2 times = 7 loops on hook, yoh and through first 6 loops and then yoh and through last 2 loops.

Row 1: Beginning in 5th ch from hook, work (1 cl, ch 3, 1 cl) in same st, *skip 4 ch, (1 cl, ch 3, 1 cl) in next st; rep from* and end with skip 2 ch, 1 dc in last st.

Row 2: Turn with ch 4, *(1 cl, ch 3, 1 cl) in ch-3 loop; rep from * and end with ch 1, 1 dc in edge st.

Repeat Row 2.

Swatch 2
STAR PATTERN

Ch 25 (or a multiple of 4 + 2 stitches in addition to the ch 3 for foundation ch)

Row 1: Begin with (3 dc, ch 1) a total of 3 times in the 6th ch from hook, *skip 3 ch, work (1 dc, ch 3) 3 times in the next ch, 1 dc in same ch; rep from * until 3 ch rem, skip 2 ch and work 1 dc in last ch.

Row 2: Ch 3, skip the first 2 dc, ch 1, 1 dc, *work (1 dc, ch 1) 3 times in the next ch loop and then 1 dc in same loop, skip 1 dc, ch 1, 2 dc, ch 1,1 dc; rep from *. End in the center of the last group, skip 1 dc, ch 1, 1 dc, work 1 dc in the 5th of the 5 ch of foundation.

Repeat Row 2, but end with 1 dc in the top of the 3 ch at beginning of row.

Swatch 3
SWEDISH WOVEN PATTERN

Multiple of 4 sts + 2 for foundation ch.

Ch 22.

Row 1: Beginning in 3rd ch from hook, work 1 sc, 2 dc, and then repeat (2 sc, 2 dc) across.
Row 2: Ch 3, 1 dc, 2 sc, work (2 dc, 2 sc) across.
Row 3: Ch 2, 1 sc, then work (2 sc, 2 dc) across.

Repeat Rows 2–3 for a total of 15 rows.

Swatch 4
CLIMBING CLUSTERS

Multiple of 8 sts + 5 ch.

Row 1: Beginning in 5th from hook, work 1 dc, *skip 3 ch, work (3 dc, ch 2, 1 dc) in next st, skip 3 ch, work (1 dc, ch 1, 1 dc) in next ch); rep from * across.
Row 2: Turn with ch 4, 1 dc in ch between dc,*(3 dc, ch 2, 1 dc) in the ch-2 loop, (1 dc, ch 1, 1 dc) in ch between dc; rep from * across.

Repeat Row 2 for pattern.

Swatch 5
LINKED DOUBLE CROCHET CLUSTERS

Linked Double Crochet: Yoh, insert hook through the st below, yoh, yarn through 2 loops on hook, yoh, insert hook through the same st as before, yoh and through 2 loops on hook, yoh and through all 3 loops on hook.

Ch 19.

Row 1: Beginning in 4th ch from hook, work 2 linked dc in each ch across.

Row 2: Ch 3, 1 dc in first 2 linked dc, work 2 linked dc in top of each group below.

Repeat Row 2 until the piece is desired size.

Swatch 6
NETTING PATTERN

Multiple of 6 ch.

Row 1: Beginning in 6th ch from hook, work 1 dc, *ch 1, skip 1 st, 1 dc, ch 1, skip 1 st, 1 dc, ch 1, 1 cl [1 cl or cluster = 1 yoh; turn work one-half turn, and bring up 1 loop around last dc, yoh, bring up 1 loop around same dc, yoh, bring up 1 loop around same dc (= 7 loops on hook), yoh and through first 6 loops, yoh and through rem 2 loops], skip 1 st, 1 dc; rep from * across.
Row 2: Turn with ch 4, *1 dc in same dc as cl,

ch 1, 1 dc in dc, ch 1, 1 cl around last dc, 1 dc in dc, ch 1; rep from * and end with 1 dc in edge st.

Row 3: Turn with ch 4, *(1 dc in dc, ch 1) 3 times, 1 cl around last worked dc; rep from * and end with 1 dc in edge st.

Swatch 7
SHELL PATTERN

Ch 27. Pattern is a multiple of 6 sts + 3 for foundation ch edge.

Row 1: Beginning in 5th ch from hook (= 1 dc + 2 ch), work *(2 dc, ch 1, 2 dc) in the same st, skip 2 ch, 1 dc, skip 2 ch; rep from * across, ending with 1 dc.

Rows 2–8: Ch 3 (= 1st dc), *(2 dc, ch 1, 2 dc) in ch loop, 1 dc in dc between shells; rep from * and end with 1 dc.

Swatch 8
LACE PATTERN

Multiple of 5 ch.

Row 1: Beginning in 4th ch from hook, 1 dc, 1 dc in 5th ch, *ch 2, skip 2 sts, 1 dc in each of next 3 sts; rep from * across.

Row 2: Turn with ch 2, 1 sc in 2nd dc, work (5 dc in the ch-2 loop, 1 sc in the center of the 3 dc) across and end with 1 sc in last dc at edge.

Row 3: Turn with ch 4, work (1 dc in 2nd dc, 1 dc in 3rd dc, 1 dc in 4th dc, ch 2) across, and end

with 3 dc, ch 1, 1 dc in edge st.

Row 4: Turn with ch 3, 2 dc in ch loop, (1 sc in 2nd dc, 5 dc in ch loop) across and end with 1 sc in 2nd dc, 3 dc in ch loop.

Row 5: Turn with ch 3, 2 dc in dc, work (ch 2, 1 dc in 2nd dc, 1 dc in 3rd dc, 1 dc in 4th dc) across and end with ch 2, 3 dc in dc.

Repeat Rows 2–5 for pattern.

Swatch 9
PEACOCK PATTERN

Chain a multiple of 10+1 sts.

Row 1: 1 sc in 2nd ch from hook, *skip 4 ch, work 9 tr in next ch, skip 4 ch, 1 sc in next ch; rep from * across.

Row 2: Begin with ch 4, 1 tr in 1st sc, *ch 3, skip 4 tr, 1 sc in next tr (= center st of the 9 tr), ch 3, skip 4 tr, 2 tr in next sc; rep from *across and end with 2 tr in last sc.

Row 3: Ch 1, 1 sc in loop between the first 2 tr, *skip 3 ch, 9 tr in next sc, skip 3 ch, 1 sc in loop between 2 tr; rep from * across. End with 1 sc in loop between the last tr and turning ch.

Repeat Rows 2 and 3 until piece is desired length.

Flower 1
BLUE ANEMONE

Flower 3
FIELD FLOWERS

Flower 2
LARGE ROSE

Flower 4
SMALL ROSE

Flower 6
VIOLET

Flower 5
SIMPLE ROSE

Flower 9
1970s FLOWER

Flower 7
BI-COLOR FLOWER

Flower 8
MARIGOLD

Flowers

HERE'S A BOUQUET OF FLOWERS WITH SEVERAL VARIETIES. FOR MOST OF THEM, WE USED MANDARIN PETIT FROM SANDNESGARN AND/OR SOME LEFTOVER YARN. WE'VE ONLY MADE COLOR SUGGESTIONS FOR EACH FLOWER.

Crochet Hook: U.S. size C-2 / 2.5 mm for all the flowers.

Flower 1
BLUE ANEMONE

Colors: Color 1, Light Purple; Color 2, Dark Purple

With Color 1, ch 4 and join into a ring with 1 sl st into 1st ch.

Rnd 1: Ch 2, 9 sc around ring and join with 1 sl st into 2nd ch. Cut yarn and change to Color 2.

Rnd 2: *(Ch 2, 3 dc, 1 sc in same sc), 1 sl st into next sc; rep from * around = 5 flower petals. Cut yarn and fasten off.

Flower 2
LARGE ROSE

Colors: Color 1, Cerise; Color 2, Light Purple; Color 3, Dark Purple; Color 4, Medium Purple
With Color 1, ch 7 and join into a ring with 1 sl st into 1st ch.

Rnd 1: Ch 3, 17 dc around ring and join with 1 sl st into top of ch 3.

Rnd 2: Change to Color 2. Work (1 sc, ch 3, skip 2 sts) 6 times = 6 ch loops. End with 1 sl st into 1st sc.

Rnd 3: 1 sl st into ch loop. In each of the ch-3 loops, work (1 sc, 5 dc, 1 sc).

Rnd 4: Change to Color 3. Work (1 sc behind petal in sc of 2nd rnd, ch 5) 6 times = 6 ch loops. End with 1 sl st into ch loop.

Rnd 5: In each of the ch-5 loops, work (1 sc, 7 dc, 1 sc).

Rnd 6: Change to Color 4. Work (1 sc behind and between petals, ch 7) 6 times and end with 1 sl st into 1st sc.

Rnd 7: In each of the ch-7 loops, work (1 sc, 9 dc, 1 sc).

Rnd 8: Change to Color 2. Work (1 sc behind and between petals, ch 9) 6 times and end with 1 sl st into 1st sc.

Rnd 9: In each of the ch-9 loops, work (1 sc, 11 dc, 1 sc). End with 1 sl st into 1st sc. Weave in all ends on WS.

Flower 3
FIELD FLOWERS

Colors: Use 2 colors of your own choosing for each flower.

With Color 1, ch 4 and join into a ring with 1 sl st into 1st ch.

Rnd 1: Ch 1, work 7 sc around ring and end with 1 sl st into 1st ch.

Rnd 2: Change to Color 2. Work (ch 5, 1 sl st into same sc, 1 sl st into next sc) around for a total of 7 petals.
Weave in all ends on WS.

Flower 4
SMALL ROSE

Color: Deep Rose

Ch 4 and join into a ring with 1 sl st into 1st ch.

Rnd 1: Ch 3, 14 dc around ring and join with 1 sl st into top of ch 3 = 15 dc total.

Rnd 2: (Ch 5, skip 2 dc, 1 sc) around = 5 ch loops. End with 1 sl st into 1st ch.

Rnd 3: Work (1 sc, 6 dc, 1 sc) in each ch loop around.

Rnd 4: Fold the petals towards you and work (1 sc behind petal in sc of 2nd rnd, ch 7) around and end with 1 sl st into 1st sc.

Rnd 5: In each of the ch-7 loops, work (1 sc, 10 dc, 1 sc). End with 1 sl st into 1st sc of Rnd 4. Cut yarn and fasten off.

Flower 5
SIMPLE ROSE

Color: Rose

Ch 6 and join into a ring with 1 sl st into 1st ch.

Rnd 1: Ch 3, 2 dc, work (ch 6, 1 sl st into last dc, 3 dc) 5 times and end with ch 6, 1 sl st into same dc, 1 sl st into top of ch 3 = 6 ch loops.

Rnd 2: (1 sl st into next dc, 11 dc around ch-6 loop) 6 times and end with 1 sl st into center dc. Cut yarn and fasten off.

Flower 6
VIOLET

Colors: 3 shades of purple as Colors 1, 2, and 3

Each flower consists of 5 petals in 3 colors.

1ST PETAL
With Color 1, ch 5 and join into a ring with 1 sl st into 1st ch.

Row 1: Ch 3 (= 1st dc) and work 6 dc around ring = 7 dc total; turn.

Row 2: Ch 5, *1 tr in next dc but omit last step, yoh and through the 3 loops on hook, 1 dc in next st; rep from * once more, ch 5, join with 1 sl st into last dc. Cut yarn and fasten off. Turn petal.

2ND PETAL
Worked in the same ring.

Row 1: Change to Color 2, attaching it with 1 sl st into ring. Ch 2 (= 1st dc), work 4 dc in ring = 5 dc total; turn.

Row 2: Ch 4, (1 dc in next dc but omit last step) 3 times, yoh and through 4 loops on hook at same time = 3 dc group, ch 4, 1 sl st into 2nd ch at beginning of Row 1. Cut yarn and fasten off.

3RD PETAL
Work as for 2nd petal, into the same ring and with the same color.

4TH PETAL
Row 1: Change to Color 3, attaching it with 1 sl st between the 1st and 2nd petals. Ch 4 (in loop behind piece), attach with 1 sl st between the 1st

and 3rd petals (behind piece), ch 2 (= 1 sc), 6 sc around ch loop = 7 sc total; turn.

Row 2: Ch 2, 1 sc in same st, 1sc in each of next 5 sts, 2 sc in last st.

Row 3: Ch 3, 1 sc in same st, 1 sc in each of next 7 sts, 2 sc in last st.

Row 4: Ch 3, (1 dc in next dc but omit last step) 4 times, yoh and through 5 loops on hook at same time = 4 dc group, ch 3, 1 sl st into next dc, ch 3; rep from * and end with ch 3, attach with 1 sl st into 3rd ch on Row 3.

Finish by embroidering, with your choice of color, a few stitches at the center of the flower (see photo). Weave in all ends neatly on WS.

Flower 7
BI-COLOR FLOWER

Colors: 2 shades of purple for Colors 1 and 2

With Color 1, ch 4 and join into a ring with 1 sl st into 1st ch.

Rnd 1: Ch 1 and work 9 sc around ring = 10 sc total.

Rnd 2: Ch 3, 1 dc in same st, and then work 2 dc in each sc around; end with 1 sl st into top of ch 3 = 20 dc.

Rnd 3: Change to Color 2. Ch 3 (= 1st dc), work 6 dc in same st, then work (skip 1 dc, 1 sl st into next dc, skip 1 dc, 7 dc in next dc) around. End with skip 1 dc, 1 sl st into next dc and 1 sl st into top of ch 3 at beginning of rnd.

Cut yarn and fasten off.

Flower 8
MARIGOLD

Color: Choose your favorite color

Ch 7 and join into a ring with 1 sl st into 1st ch.

Rnd 1: Ch 2 (= 1st sc) and work 19 sc around ring = 20 sc total. End with 1 sl st into top of ch 2 at beginning of rnd.

Rnd 2: (Ch 3, 1 tr in each of next 3 sts, ch 3, 1 sl st into next sc) 5 times and end with 1 sl st into 1st ch at beginning of rnd = 5 petals. Cut yarn and fasten off.

Flower 9
1970s FLOWER

Colors: Color 1, Purple; Color 2, Pink

With Color 1, ch 4 and join into a ring with 1 sl st into 1st ch.

Rnd 1: Ch 1 (= 1st sc) and work 6 sc around ring = 7 sc total; end with 1 sl st into 1st ch.

Rnd 2: Ch 1, 1 sc in same st and then 2 sc in each sc around. End with 1 sl st into 1st ch = 14 sc total.

Rnd 3: Ch 1, 1 sc in same st, (1 sc into next st, 2 sc in next st) around = 20 sc; end with 1 sl st into 1st ch.

Rnd 4: Change to Color 2. Ch 1, 1 sc in same st, (1 dc in next st, 2 dc in next sc, 1 dc, 2 sc in next sc) around; end with 1 sl st into 1st ch.

Rnd 5: Ch 1, 1 sc in same st, (1 dc in next st, 2 dc in next st, 2 dc in next st, 1 dc, 2 sc) around; end with 1 sl st into 1st ch. Cut yarn and weave in all ends on WS.

Edging 1
PICOT WITH DOUBLE CROCHET

Edging 2
PICOT WITH CHAIN STITCH

Edging 3
LARGE FANS

Edging 4
CRAB STITCH

Edging 5
SMALL WAVES

Edging 6
SMALL FANS

Edgings

FINISHED PROJECTS CAN BE EDGED IN MANY DIFFERENT WAYS.
HERE ARE A FEW GOOD SUGGESTIONS.

If you are working around a piece, repeat the pattern all the way around. Always begin the edging where it will be least visible—for example, at the center of the side, back neck, centered under a sleeve, etc. That way, if you cannot work complete repeats around, it will not be noticed. On a blanket or coverlet, it is not easy to hide incomplete repeats, so try to adjust the pattern as you get near the end of the round. Some of the patterns are enhanced with one round (or several) in single crochet before you work the edging. A round of single crochet can also serve as an edging.

Edging 1
PICOTS (with double crochet)

Attach yarn with 1 sl st; work (ch 3, 1 dc in 3rd ch from hook, skip 2 sts, 1 sc in next st) around.

Edging 2
PICOTS (with chain stitches)

Row 1: Sc in each st.

Row 2: 1 sl st, (ch 3, 1 sc in sl st, 1 sl st in next st) across/around.

Edging 3
LARGE FANS

Attach yarn with 1 sl st, work 1 sc, (skip 2 sts, 5 dc in next st, skip 2 sts, 1 sc in next st) across/around.

Edging 4
CRAB STITCH

Crab st is simply single crochet worked backwards, from left to right. Attach yarn with 1 sc. *Insert hook into next st to the right, yoh and bring yarn through, yoh and through both loops on hook; rep from *.

Edging 5
SMALL WAVES

Attach yarn with 1 sl st on edge, (ch 3, 1 dc in next st, 1 sl st into next st) across/around.
   This edging is used for the potholder with field flowers.

Edging 7
PICOTS WITH CRAB STITCH AND
SINGLE CROCHET

Edging 8
SMALL CHAIN STITCH LOOPS

Edging 9
FAN BOUQUETS

Edging 6

SMALL FANS

Attach yarn with 1 sl st on edge, ch 3 and work
2 dc in same st, (skip 1 st, 1 sl st into next st,
skip 1 st, 3 dc in next st) across/around and end
with 1 sl st.

Edging 7

PICOTS
(with crab stitch and single crochet)

Attach yarn with 1 sl st on edge, (ch 3, 1 sl st
into 1st ch, 1 sl st into next st, 1 sc in next st)
across/around.

Edging 8

SMALL CHAIN STITCH LOOPS

Attach yarn with 1 sc on edge, (ch 3, skip 1 st, 1
sc in next st) across/around.

Edging 9

FAN BOUQUETS

Attach yarn with 1 sl st in corner, ch 3, [skip 2
or 3 sts, work (2 dc, ch 1, 2 dc) in next st] across/
around and end with ch 3, 1 sl st into end of
piece.
This edging was made around the white baby
blanket on page 21.

A little
CROCHET
SCHOOL

While many people are familiar with handling a crochet hook and are experienced at various techniques, there are others who need help and guidance. The Crochet School here illustrates the details for beginners and more advanced crocheters. The information will also be useful for other projects, not just those in this book.

Short Crochet Course

Please note that U.S. terms are used in this book. For the equivalent British terms, see Abbreviations.

CHAIN STITCH (ch) and foundation chain. Most crochet projects begin with a foundation of chain stitches.

❶ Begin with a slip knot in the yarn. Place the loop on the hook. The first loop is not included in the stitch count. Hold the yarn over your left index finger.

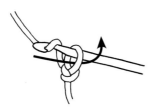

❷ Bring the yarn through the loop on the hook.

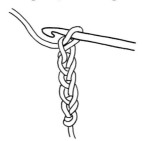

❸ Continue to make chain stitches the same way (yarn around hook and through loop on hook) until you have a chain.

SLIP STITCH (sl st)

❶ Begin with a foundation chain. Insert the hook into the front of the 2nd st from the hook.

❷ Yarn around hook and through the two loops on the hook. Repeat Steps 1 and 2 across.

SINGLE CROCHET (sc)

❶ Begin with a foundation chain. Insert the hook into the front of the 2nd st from the hook, yarn around hook and through stitch.

❷ Yarn around hook and through the two loops on the hook. Repeat Steps 1 and 2.

HALF DOUBLE CROCHET (hdc)

❶ Begin with a foundation chain. Yarn around hook and insert the hook into the 3rd st from the hook, yarn around hook and bring yarn through.

❷ Yarn around hook and through the 3 loops on the hook. Repeat Steps 1 and 2 across/around.

DOUBLE CROCHET (dc)

❶ Begin with a foundation chain. Yarn around hook and insert the hook into the 4th st from the hook, yarn around hook and bring yarn through.

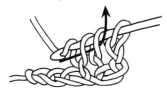

❷ Yarn around hook and through the first 2 loops on the hook. Yarn around hook and through the remaining 2 loops on hook.

❸ Repeat Steps 1 and 2 across/around.

TREBLE CROCHET (tr)

❶ Begin with a foundation chain. Yarn around hook twice and insert the hook into the 5th st from the hook, yarn around hook and bring yarn through.

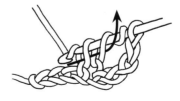

❷ (Yarn around hook and through the first 2 loops on the hook) three times.

❸ Repeat Steps 1 and 2 across/around.

DOUBLE TREBLE (dbl tr)

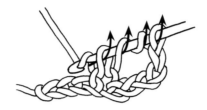

❷ (Yarn around hook and through the first 2 loops on the hook) four times.

❶ Begin with a foundation chain. Yarn around hook three times and insert the hook into the 6th st from the hook, yarn around hook and bring yarn through.

❸ Repeat Steps 1 and 2 across/around.

Various Ways to Begin

A project can begin with a foundation chain as shown on page 144 or as shown below.

SINGLE CROCHET FOUNDATION CHAIN

❶ Make a slip knot and ch 2. Insert the hook through the 1st chain st, yarn around hook and through.

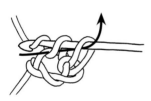

❷ Yarn around hook and through both loops on hook. Repeat Steps 1 and 2.

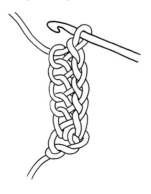

BEGIN WITH A RING (Magic Ring)

Begin with a ring of yarn that the stitches will be worked around. The piece can be crocheted around as a flat circle or as a cord that can be shifted to a rectangle, square, or hexagon. This method is helpful when you need to later close the circle because you can pull the yarn tail to tighten the piece.

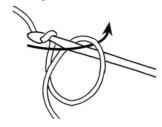

❶ Make a circle of yarn as pictured. Insert the crochet hook, yarn around hook and through the ring, yarn around hook and through the loop on the hook.

❷ Work the number of single crochet sts specified in the pattern around the ring. Make sure you encase both strands of the ring as you work.

❸ Use the loose end of the ring to pull the circle closed. End round of single crochet with a slip stitch into the first single crochet.

Gauge Swatch

Before starting a project, you should always make a swatch to test the gauge. A gauge swatch is necessary so you can change to a smaller or larger hook in case your gauge doesn't match that given in the pattern.

HOW TO MAKE A GAUGE SWATCH

The gauge swatch should be slightly larger than a 4 x 4 in / 10 x 10 cm square. Lay the swatch flat and count the stitches across and rows up in 4 in / 10 cm. Compare your stitch and row counts with those given in the pattern. If you have more stitches than specified, change to a larger size hook. If you have fewer stitches, change to a smaller size hook.

HOW TO COUNT THE STITCHES

Count the single crochet (or other stitches) as shown in the drawing below.

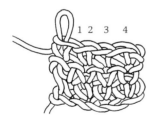

Increasing Stitches

The easiest way to increase is to work two stitches into the same stitch, either at the beginning or end of a row or in both places. You can also increase within the row/round.

INCREASING ONE STITCH AT EACH SIDE

Make the same stitch twice into the first and last stitches of the row.

INCREASING ONE STITCH WITHIN THE ROW/ROUND

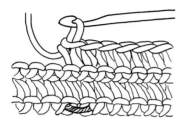

Make the same stitch twice into one stitch of the row/round below.

INCREASING TWO STITCHES

Make the same stitch three times into one stitch of the row/round below.

Increasing Several Stitches

If you are instructed to increase several stitches at the sides, make a line of chain stitches.

INCREASING AT THE BEGINNING OF A ROW

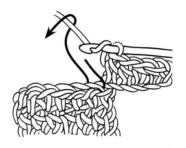

Make as many chain stitches as needed for the increase + turning st(s). Turn and work the new stitches into the chain.

INCREASING AT THE END OF A ROW

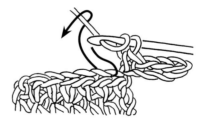

So that the new stitches will all be at the same level on both sides, make the crochet chain at the end of a row before increasing at the beginning of a row.

❶ Chain the number of stitches specified in the pattern + turning chain. Work in slip stitches over the new chain stitches.

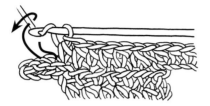

❷ On the next row, work the new stitches into the slip stitches of previous row.

Decreasing Stitches

The easiest way to decrease stitches is to skip a stitch at the beginning or end of a row or in both places, or by skipping a stitch within a row. You can also join two stitches or omit stitches at the beginning or end of a row.

DECREASING ONE STITCH AT BEGINNING AND END OF A ROW

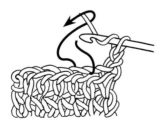

Beginning of Row: Work turning chain, skip 1 stitch, work next stitch.
End of Row: Skip the next-to-last stitch and work the last stitch.

DECREASING SEVERAL STITCHES AT BEGINNING AND END OF A ROW

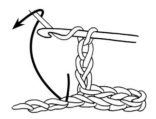

Beginning of Row: Slip stitch over the given number of stitches to be omitted; work turning chain and continue in pattern.
End of Row: Do not work the given number of stitches to be omitted; work turning chain.

DECREASING WITHIN THE PIECE

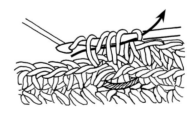

Join two stitches. Place a stitch marker or strand of yarn where the decreases are to be made.

CROCHET TWO STITCHES TOGETHER

The instructions below describe joining stitches at the sides or within a row/round.

Single Crochet

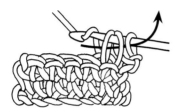

Turn with ch 1, insert hook into 1st stitch, *yarn around hook and through stitch. Work from * in next stitch, yarn around hook and through all 3 loops on hook.

Double Crochet

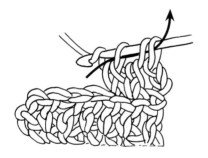

Turn with ch 3, *yarn around hook, insert hook through 1st stitch and bring yarn through. Yarn around hook and through 2 loops on hook. Repeat from * on next st and then yarn around hook and through remaining 3 loops on hook.

HALF DOUBLE CROCHET

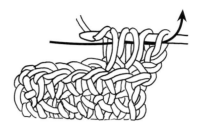

Turn with ch 2, *yarn around hook, insert hook through 1st stitch and bring yarn through. Repeat from * on next st and then yarn around hook and through all 5 loops on hook.

Turning Chain (tc)

Stitches vary in height and width and make each project distinctive. Each row is is the foundation for the next row to be worked.

When moving from one row to the next, you need to make one or more chain stitches to begin the new row so the piece won't pull in at the sides. The turning chain substitutes for the first stitch of the row.

SLIP STITCHES

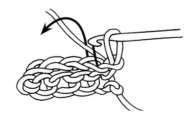

Turn with 1 ch. Insert hook in back loop of the first stitch of previous row.

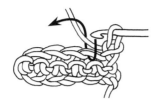

SINGLE CROCHET

Turn with 1 ch (in some instances, you might turn with ch 2 for single crochet). Insert the hook under both stitch loops of the first stitch of previous row.

HALF DOUBLE CROCHET

Turn with ch 2. Work 1 half double crochet in the first stitch of previous row.

Double Crochet: Turn with ch 3.
Treble Crochet: Turn with ch 4.
Double Treble Crochet: Turn with ch 5.

Carrying and Catching in Ends

If you are crocheting small motifs in two colors, cover the yarn not being used at the same time as working the stitches by holding (carrying) yarn along top of previous row. Vertical and horizontal stripes require a separate little ball for each stripe.

NEW YARN, SINGLE CROCHET

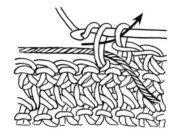

❶ Lay the new yarn along the top edge of previous row and work over it until needed.

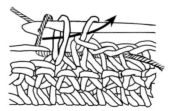

❷ When changing colors, work the last step of the previous stitch with the new color. If you will continue with the old yarn as part of the motif, carry and cover it as before. If you do not need the old yarn, carry and cover it for a few stitches and then cut it.

NEW YARN, DOUBLE CROCHET

❶ Lay the new color along the top edge of previous row. Yarn around hook with old color and insert hook into next stitch.

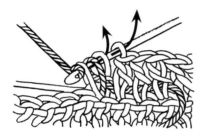

❷ Yarn around hook with both colors and through stitch. Yarn around hook with new color and complete double crochet.

❸ Carry and catch the old color along top edge. When changing colors, work the last step of the double crochet with the new color.

Crocheting in the Round

If you want a flat circle, you need to increase with a specific system, depending on whether you are working with single or double crochet stitches. If the pattern does not specify a particular way to increase, you can use the methods below. If the circle starts to buckle, you should skip a round of increases. If the outer edge folds up, work a round without any increases.

SINGLE CROCHET

Ch 4 and join into a ring with 1 sl st into 1st ch (see page 144). Begin every round with ch 1 (= 1st sc) and end each rnd with 1 sl st into 1st ch.

Rnd 1: Work 8 sc around ring.

Rnd 2: Work 2 sc in each sc around = 16 sc.

Rnd 3: Work (1 sc in next sc, 2 sc into next st) around = 24 sc.

Rnd 4: Work (1 sc in each of next 2 sc, 2 sc into next st) around = 32 sc.

Rnd 5: Work (1 sc in each of next 3 sc, 2 sc into next st) around = 40 sc.
Continue, increasing 8 sts on every round, with 1 more sc between each increase.

DOUBLE CROCHET

Begin with a magic ring (see page 147); join into a ring with 1 sl st. Begin every round with ch 3 (= 1st dc) and end each rnd with 1 sl st into top of ch 3

Rnd 1: Work 12 dc around ring.

Rnd 2: Work 2 dc in each dc around = 16 dc.

Rnd 3: Work (1 dc in next dc, 2 dc into next st) around = 24 dc.

Rnd 4: Work (1 dc in each of next 2 dc, 2 dc into next st) around = 36 dc.

Rnds 5–10: Work [1 dc in each of next 3 dc (on Rnd 5 and then into next 4, 5, 6, 7, 8 dc on subsequent rounds), 2 dc into next st] around. Make sure the size of the circle is correct. If so, cut yarn and fasten off. If you want a larger circle, continue, increasing 8 sts on every round, with 1 more dc between each increase.

CROCHETING AROUND IN A SPIRAL

If you want to crochet around in a spiral, increase as described above but do not end round with a slip stitch. The circle will look smoothest if the increases are not stacked above each other but are offset slightly. Place a marker at the beginning of the round and move it up as you work.

THE FIRST STITCH WHEN CROCHETING AROUND

On pages 151 and 152, you'll find an overview of how many chain stitches are needed for turning on rows back and forth. So that your work will be even, the first stitch of the round should also be substituted with an appropriate number of chain stitches.

THE LAST STITCH WHEN CROCHETING AROUND

In a pattern that ends a round with an ordinary stitch, you usually close the round with 1 slip stitch in top of the chain at beginning of round.

Variations of the Most Common Stitches

By inserting the hook differently than usual for a stitch, you can easily affect the stitches because the yarn is twisted in a different direction.

CROSSED SINGLE CROCHET

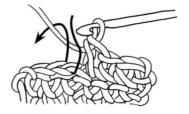

Work as for regular single crochet but the hook goes over the yarn when making the yarnover.

CROSSED DOUBLE CROCHET

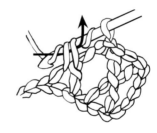

Make a foundation chain of a suitable length. Yarn around hook twice, insert hook in the 6th chain from hook and bring yarn through, yarn around hook and bring through 2 loops. * Yarn around hook, skip 1 st, insert hook in next st, yarn around hook and through 2 loops at a time (= 4 times), ch 1, work 1 dc in center of cross just worked (= crossed double crochet is complete), yarn around hook twice, insert hook into next st, yarn around hook and though 2 loops, etc at a time; repeat from *.

RIB OR PLISSÉ CROCHET

Work into back loops only for a rib effect on right side and into front loops for a ribbed effect on the wrong side.

WORKING BETWEEN STITCHES

Insert hook in the space between two stitches of previous row.

INSERT HOOK INTO STITCHES TWO ROWS BELOW

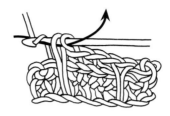

Insert the hook in the space between two stitches, two rows below.

RELIEF STITCHES (FRONT AND BACK POST DOUBLE CROCHET)

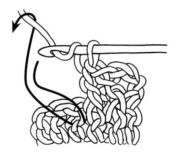

Insert the hook from the front around the post of a double crochet or from the back around the post of a double crochet.

BOBBLES

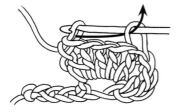

Work 5 double crochet stitches into the same stitch. Remove hook from last loop and insert it into the loop of 1st dc and then into last dc of the 5 dc, yarn around hook and through the loops on hook.

BOUILLON STITCHES

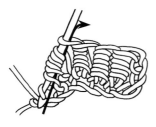

Wrap the yarn around the hook several times; insert the hook through a stitch loop on previous row. Yarn around hook and through all the loops on hook.

DOUBLE CROCHET AROUND DOUBLE CROCHET

Yarn around hook, insert hook from back to front, around the double crochet and out the back again; make 1 dc.

CRAB STITCH

Crab st is simply single crochet worked backwards, from left to right. Attach yarn with 1 sc. *Insert hook into next st to the right, yarn around hook and bring yarn through, yarn around hook and through both loops on hook; rep from *.

PICOTS

Picots are worked along an edge: (Ch 3, insert hook into 1st ch and make 1 sc, 1 sc in next st) across/around.

Tunisian Crochet

Tunisian crochet (sometimes called Afghan crochet) is worked back and forth in a two-step sequence. On the first or forward pass, loops are picked up across a row and retained on the hook. On the next row, the return pass, the loops are worked off, one after the other. The work is not turned but always faces you. You'll need a special long hook for Tunisian crochet.

❶ Work from right to left. *Insert hook into 1 stitch, yarn around hook and through stitch; repeat from * across.

❷ Work from left to right. Yarn around hook and through the first loop on the hook, *yarn around hook and through 2 loops; repeat from * across.

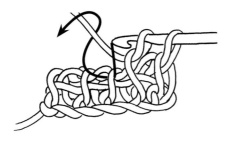

❸ When working from right to left, insert the hook through the vertical loop of the stitch on the previous row.
Repeat Steps 1 and 2.

Loop Crochet

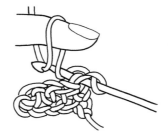

❶ Wrap the yarn around your left index finger, insert hook into the 1st stitch through both loops.

❷ Bring the yarn through; slip yarn off finger, yarn around hook. Bring yarn through the 3 loops on hook.

❸ Repeat Steps 1 and 2 across the row. Work 1 row of single crochet before the next loop row.

Peacock Crochet

For peacock crochet, you'll need a super large knitting needle (U.S. size 50 / 25 mm and crochet hook U.S. size L-11 / 7 mm).

Chain the number of stitches specified in the pattern. Place the last stitch onto the knitting needle. Bring up a loop through each of the chain stitches and place the loops one after the other on the knitting needle (figure 1).

Let the first 5 loops slide off the needle and twist them a quarter turn to the right so they lay over each other (figure 2). Secure the loops at the top with 1 sc and then work 5 sc into the loops (figure 3). Repeat across (figure 4).

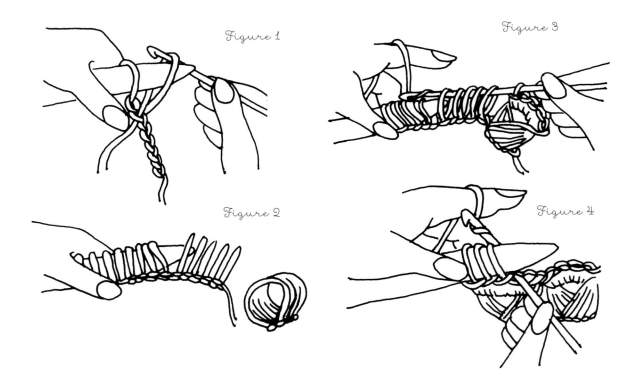

Figure 1

Figure 3

Figure 2

Figure 4

A LITTLE CROCHET SCHOOL

Net Crochet

The open work of net crochet is achieved by making a large number of chain stitches between the joining stitches. You can vary the netting by the number of stitches used and the distance between them.

NETTING WITH CHAIN STITCH HOLES

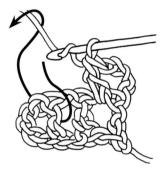

Insert the hook into the space or loop by chain stitches of the previous row.

FILET CROCHET

Work 1 dc, *ch 2, skip 2 sts of previous row, 1 dc in next st; repeat from *.

DOUBLE CROCHET AND CORDS

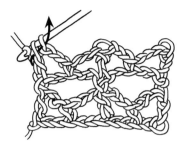

*1 dc, ch 3, skip 2 sts of previous row, 1 sc in next st, ch 3, skip 2 sts; repeat from *.

DIAGONAL NETTING

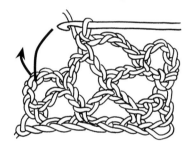

*Work 1 sc in the center of a 5-ch loop of previous row, ch 5; repeat from *.

Tapestry Crochet

Tapestry crochet is a technique often used for mittens by many generations. The technique makes tight stitches for warmer mittens.

The technique is very easy: crochet around in a spiral with slip stitches worked only through back loops on every round.

Granny Squares

BELOVED PATTERNS HAVE MANY NAMES AND GRANNY SQUARES ARE SOMETIMES ALSO CALLED GREAT GRANDMOTHER'S SQUARES IN SOME TRADITIONS. NO MATTER WHICH NAME YOU USE, THESE SQUARES HAVE PASSED THE TEST OF TIME.

Granny squares can be varied in so many ways, especially with the use of color. The basic pattern is simple and the squares can be joined for larger and smaller projects, parts of garments, coverlets, blankets, runners, and so much more. A large square can become a vest or cover a pillow. A small square can be used as an eye-catcher on a garment or cover a hole or stain.

BASIC INSTRUCTIONS

If you are changing colors, when working the slip stitch at the end of the round, work it with the new color.

Ch 6 and join into a ring with 1 sl st into 1st ch.

Rnd 1: Ch 3, work 2 dc around ring, (ch 3, 3 dc around ring) 3 times, ch 3 and end with 1 sl st into top of ch 3.

Rnd 2: Ch 3, 2 dc in same loop (corner), *ch 1, (3 dc, ch 3, 3 dc) in next ch loop; repeat from * 2 more times and end with ch 1, (3 dc, ch 3) in corner and join with 1 sl st into top of ch 3.

Rnd 3: Ch 3, 2 dc in same loop (corner), *ch 1, 3 dc in ch-1 loop, ch 1, (3 dc, ch 3, 3 dc) in ch-3 loop at corner; repeat from * 2 more times and end with ch 1, 3 dc in ch-1 loop, ch 1, 3 dc in last corner, ch 3 and join with 1 sl st into top of ch 3.

Rnd 4: Ch 3, 2 dc in same loop (corner), *(ch 1, 3 dc in ch-1 loop) 2 times, ch 1 (3 dc, ch 3, 3 dc) in ch-3 loop at corner; repeat from * 2 more times and end with (ch 1, 3 dc in ch-1 loop) 2 times, in last corner, work 3 dc, ch 3 and join with 1 sl st into top of ch 3.

Continue the same way, with 1 more 3-dc group along each side on every round, until the square is desired size.

Finishing Your Project

FASTENING OFF YARN

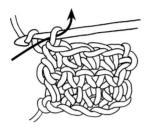

❶ After the last stitch has been worked, cut the yarn, leaving a tail about 6 in / 15 cm long. Bring the end through the last stitch loop.

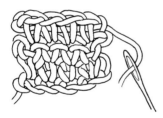

❷ Thread the end into a tapestry needle and weave the end through a few stitches on the wrong side.

EDGES AND JOINING

Crocheted pieces can be joined with yarn threaded through a blunt tapestry needle. Sew the pieces together by hand with back stitch.

Joining with single crochet makes a much stronger join. Often the single crochet is worked with a contrasting color yarn with the right side of the fabric facing you.

Sample to see whether crochet or sewing will look best on both sides before you do all the joining.

Back Stitch
Place the two pieces with right side facing right side and pin together. Sew with evenly spaced back stitches.

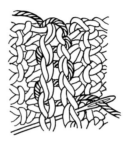

Simple Mattress Stitch
Place the pieces with the wrong side up and the edges abutting. Use small back and forth mattress stitches along the edges. This makes a flat seam.

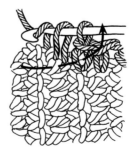

Single Crochet Stitches
Insert the hook through the piece one stitch in from the edge and work single crochet through both layers.

Design Your Own Patterns

The easiest way to design your own patterns is to start from the instructions for the type of garment you are thinking about making, such as a cardigan. Begin by making a little gauge swatch in the pattern given in the instructions. Now extend the gauge swatch by working a motif you like. Check to see if the gauge is the same with both patterns. Follow the instructions for the length of the garment.

If you don't have a pattern that you can adapt, you can sketch the garment you want to crochet. Cut out a simple pattern with lines as straight as possible. You'll need a motif for the front and back plus the sleeves. If the garment has pockets, it's a good idea to begin with them and use the pockets as gauge swatches. Lay the paper pattern on the table and place the crochet swatch over it. Measure and calculate how many stitches you need for the foundation chain. Make sure the total stitch count is a multiple of the pattern stitches. Study some of the simple patterns in the book for help with this.

Abbreviations in the Instructions

So that the patterns won't be too long and complicated, abbreviations are used. Try and learn the most important words and phrases to make reading the instructions easier. The crocheting will be faster and you'll be less likely to make mistakes if you can read the instructions and abbreviations.

ABBREVIATIONS

beg	begin, beginning
ch	chain
cl	cluster
cm	centimeter(s)
dc	double crochet (British: treble crochet)
dtr	double treble (British: triple treble)
gr	group
hdc	half double crochet (British: half treble crochet)
in	inch(es)
m	meter(s)
mm	millimeter(s)
pm	place marker
rem	remain(s)(ing)
rep	repeat
rnd(s)	round(s)
RS	right side
sc	single crochet (British: double crochet)
sl	slip
st(s)	stitch(es)
tr	treble (British: double treble)
trtr	triple treble (British: quadruple treble)
WS	wrong side
yd	yard(s)
yoh	yarn over hook, also yarn around hook

Other important phrases

Chain loop (ch loop) = a row of chain stitches over a crocheted row and which will have other stitches worked into it on the following row.

A stitch loop has two halves: the first, front loop, is one of the two strands of a stitch lying nearest the front of the work and the other, the back loop, is the strand further away. The instructions will usually indicate whether to work in both loops or the front or back loops only. Usually, if not specified, work through both loops.

Repeats

* = the stitches following an asterisk are to be worked in sequence as many times as indicated in the instructions (indicated by "repeat from * x number of times").

( ) = a stitch sequence within parentheses should be worked as many times as indicated just outside the close parenthesis. For example, (2 dc, ch 1) 5 times means that you work the sequence 2 dc, ch 1 5 times total.

Washing and Care of Crocheted Garments

Follow the washing instructions given on the yarn ball band.

NOTE:
- Crocheted pieces should be washed with the wrong side out.
- A multi-color piece should not be soaked.
- Wash at the recommended water temperature and do not add too much washing soap.
- Do not use washing soap with bleach unless washing pure, white cotton.

- After the washing cycle is complete, do not leave crocheted pieces in the washer; immediately put them out to dry.
- Lay piece(s) out flat and pat to finished measurements and leave until completely dry. Do not dry in strong sunlight or heat.
- Store crocheted pieces flat, not hanging.

WASHING SYMBOLS

 Do not wash

 Machine wash at 86°F / 30°C in gentle cycle

 Hand wash

 Machine wash at 104°F / 40°C

 Machine wash at 104°F / 40°C and use spin cycle. Half-full machine

 Machine wash at 140°F / 60°C

 Chlorine bleach can be used

 Do not use chlorine bleach

 Cannot tolerate rinse water stronger than perchloroethylene

 Do not rinse

 Iron, high heat, maximum 392°F / 200°C

 Iron, medium heat, maximum 302°F / 150°C

 Iron, low heat, maximum 230°F / 110°C

 Do not iron

 Tumble dry (medium heat)

 Tumble dry (low heat)

 Do not tumble dry

 Line dry

 Drip dry

 Dry flat

STIFFENING AND STARCHING CROCHET WORK

The most common way to stiffen or starch doilies, runners, birthday crowns, Christmas decorations, etc, is to use a sugar solution or a confectioner's sugar glaze. A third choice is carpet glue. Here are some suggestions for all three options.

Sugar solution: Bring about ¾–1¼ cup / 2–3 dl water to boil (the amount depends on how much you will be starching). Take off heat and add 6 tablespoons–¾ cup / 1–2 dl sugar and stir until sugar begins dissolving. Add 6 tablespoons–¾ cup / 1–2 dl cold water. Let cool until lukewarm.

Confectioner's sugar glaze: Pour some confectioner's sugar into a deep bowl. Slowly stir in water until mixture is a thick paste.

Carpet Glue: Mix carpet glue with water until it is a thick paste (or follow the instructions on the packet).

Now stiffen the crochet work as follows:
Dip the piece into the starch or paste. Wring out piece and use paper toweling to wipe away any excess paste. Lay the piece flat or upright to dry on baking parchment paper.

If the piece has to be shaped in a particular way, you can support it with pins or shewers on a wooden plate or bowl. If necessary, you can turn the bowl upside down and spread the piece on it so that it won't collapse.

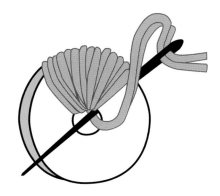

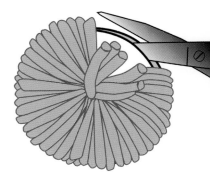

Embellishments

POMPOMS

Pompoms can be made in various sizes depending on how they will be used. Tie small pompoms to the ends of tie cords and large ones on the tops of hats.

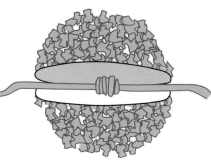

For a medium pompom, cut out two circles about 1½ in / 4 cm in diameter from heavy cardstock. You can use a small glass to draw the circle. Now draw a small circle, about ⅜ in / 1 cm in diameter in the center of each of the larger circles. Cut out the circles and place them one atop the other. Wind yarn around the circles until they are full. Insert sharp scissor tips between the circles and clip open. Firmly tie a strong thread (linen thread works well) between the circles. Remove the paper circles. Trim pompom with scissors. Roll the pompom between your hands and fluff it by carefully holding the pompom over some steam. Use the thread from the center of the pompom to attach it.

TASSELS

Cut a piece of heavy cardstock or cardboard as wide as you'd like the tassel's length. Wrap yarn around the template. Tie a strong thread around the yarn at the top. Cut open the lower ends of the yarn. Tie thread or yarn around the tassel about ⅜–¾ in / 1–2 cm from the top. Attach the tassel with the same thread or yarn wrapping the top of the tassel.

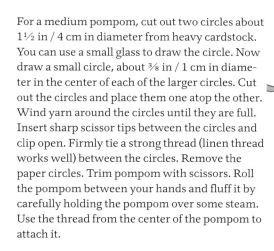

Yarn

SIMILAR YARNS FROM VARIOUS COMPANIES

Some yarns can easily substitute for others because they are the same weight, are recommended for the same knitting and crochet gauge, and will produce similar size finished projects. You should always make a gauge swatch before starting any project. Swatching will let you know if you have the correct crochet gauge for an accurate result. This is especially important if you are making any substitutions. If, for example, you crochet with a hook U.S. size C-2 / 2.5 mm, you will produce a tighter gauge than if you use a U.S. size D-3 / 3 mm hook. The lists given here will help you make the best substitutions although there may still be some differences between the various yarns. If you can't find the yarn we've recommended, it is quite likely that you can find a similar size yarn from other yarn producers. If you live in Norway, you should have access to most of the yarns recommended in the book. We couldn't include every yarn from every producer, but we have listed the yarns we used and the closest qualities.

NOTE: Some of the yarns are listed in more than one group because they are suitable for various knitting and crochet gauges.

YARN COMPANIES AND THEIR YARNS

SandnesGarn: Alpaca, Mini Alpaca, Smart, Mandarin Petit, Lanett Baby Wool, Mandarin Medi, Kashmir Alpakka, Alpaca Silk, Duo, Mini Duett, Easy, Soft Alpaca, Fritidsgarn, Kitten Mohair, London gold/silver, Silk Mohair

Dale Garn: Falk,Freestyle, Dale Baby Wool, Vipe, Cotinga, Dale Alpaca, Gullfasan, Hegre, Hubro, Lerke, Lille Lerke, Daletta

Rauma: Pt Pandora, Pt Petunia, Pt Sumatra, Pt All Season Yarn, Pt 2, Pt 3, Pt 5, Iris Alpaca, Puno, Plum, Concorde (glitter thread), Metallic (gold, silver, etc)

Drops Design (Garnstudio): Alaska, Eskimo, Merino Extra Fine, Muskat, Safran, Paris, Kid Silk, Karisma, Lima, Baby Alpaca Silk, Glitter (gold, silver, etc), Vivaldi

Du Store Alpakka: Fine Alpaca (Tynn Alpakka), Faerytale, Bling effect thread (with sequins), Sterk, Baby Silk

Solberg Spinderi: Fiol

Effect threads used: London gold/silver (SandnesGarn), Concorde and Metallic gold/silver (Rauma), Bling sequin thread (Du Store Alpakka), Paillettes (sequin thread from Katia), Glitter (Drops Design).

YARNS BY WEIGHT

Crochet Hook size:

U.S. sizes C-2–D-3 / 2.5–3 mm:

Dale: Baby Ull, Alpaca, Lille Lerke, Vipe

Drops: Baby Merino, Baby Alpaca Silk, Alpaca, Safran, Kid Silk, Alpaca Silk, Mini Alpaca, Mini Duett,Mandarin Petit, Lanett Baby Wool, London gold/silver, Vivaldi

Rauma: Pt Pandora, Pt 5, Plum, Concorde

Du Store Alpakka: Fine Alpaca (Tynn Alpakka), Faerytale, Baby Silk

SandnesGarn: Silk Mohair

Solberg Spinderi: Fiol

U.S. sizes E-4–G-6 / 3.5–4 mm:

Dale Garn: Falk, Lerke, Gullfasan, Alpaca

SandnesGarn: Duo, Kitten Mohair, Smart

Drops Design: Merino Extra Fine, Karisma, Muskat, Lima

Rauma: Pt Petunia, Pt 2, Pt 5

Du Store Alpakka: Sterk, Baby Silk

U.S. sizes 7–J-9 / 4.5–5.5 mm:
Dale Garn: Cotinga, Freestyle, Hegre
Rauma: Pt All Season Yarn, Pt Sumatra, Pt 3, Iris Alpaca, Puno
Drops Design: Alaska, Lima, Paris, Nepal, Soft Alpaca,
SandnesGarn: Fritidsgarn, Kashmir Alpakka

U.S. sizes L-11–M/N-13 / 7–9 mm:
SandnesGarn: Easy
Dale Garn: Hubro
Drops: Eskimo

Suppliers

Dale of Norway
Mango Moon Yarns
info@mangomoonyarns.com
www.mangomoonyarns.com

Ingebretsen's (Rauma too)
info@ingebretsens.com
www.ingebretsens.com

Rauma Yarn
The Yarn Guys
info@theyarnguys.com
http://theyarnguys.com/

Nordic Fiber Arts
info@nordicfiberarts.com
www.nordicfiberarts.com

Sandnes Garn
Swedish Yarn Imports
PO Box 2069
Jamestown, NC 27282
800-331-5648
info@swedishyarn.com
www.swedishyarn.com

Du Store Alpakka
Du Store Alpakka
www.dustorealpakka.com

Webs – America's Yarn Store
75 Service Center Road
Northampton, MA 01060
800-367-9327
customerservice@yarn.com
www.yarn.com

If you are unable to obtain any of the yarn used in this book, it can be replaced with a yarn of a similar weight and composition. Please note, however, that the finished projects may vary slightly from those shown, depending on the yarn used. Try www.yarnsub.com for suggestions.

For more information on selecting or substituting yarn, contact your local yarn shop or an online store; they are familiar with all types of yarns and would be happy to help you. Additionally, the online knitting community at Ravelry.com has forums where you can post questions about specific yarns. Yarns come and go so quickly these days and there are so many beautiful yarns available.

Acknowledgments

Thank you to everyone who was such a super help with the crochet work: Elin Juhanak, Nina Holum, Tone Berg. Anne-Mari Nielsen, Geraldine Loose, and Selma Svendsberget.

Thank you to those who loaned us patterns: Ingrid Elfstedt Glendrange (Delicate Chevron Pattern Blanket). We also want to thank the kind customer in the shop (whose name we never discovered) who gave us the idea for the Simple Mittens.

Thank you to the following yarn companies who supplied the yarns for the book: Dale Garn AS, Drops Design (Garnstudio AS), Sandnes-Garn AS, Rauma Ullvarefabrikk and Du Store Alpakka.

We would also like to acknowledge and thank SandnesGarn, Dale Garn, and Drops Design for allowing us to use these designs in the book:

Dale Garn: Lace Scarf, Feminine Jacket, Green Hat, and Child's Dress with Crocheted Yoke.
Drops Design: Lace Pattern Cardigan and Delicate Chevron Blanket.

Thank you to May B. Langhelle for the fantastic photography and to Laila Mjøs for the beautiful layout of the book.

A big thank you to the world's best, calmest, and, not least, most patient editor, Ann Kristin Nås Gjerde. She has been a huge help, both practical and creative. Many of the ideas are thanks to her!

Our biggest thanks go to Synnøve Smedal without whom there would be no book. We want to thank her once more for working with us and keeping us in line. Her orderly work methods and effectiveness are enviable and highly prized!

Another big thanks to all our models.